The Worlds We Live In

The Editors

Claire Foster is Lay Canon at St Paul's Cathedral and Deputy Director of the St Paul's Institute. She is Policy Advisor to the Church of England on science, medicine, technology and environmental issues.

Edmund Newell is Chancellor of St Paul's Cathedral and Director of the St Paul's Institute. He was formerly a Research Fellow in Economic History at Nuffield College, Oxford.

St Paul's Institute

St Paul's Institute was founded in 2002 as a public forum for reflection, debate and education on the spiritual and ethical challenges of our times. It aims to foster a Christian response to questions facing business, finance and global economics, including environmental, social and political issues, and to influence opinion, both in the Christian world and beyond.

www.stpauls.co.uk/institute
020–74891011

The Worlds We Live In

Dialogues with Rowan Williams
on Global Economics and Politics

Edited by
Claire Foster and Edmund Newell

First published in 2005 by
Darton, Longman and Todd Ltd
1 Spencer Court
140–142 Wandsworth High Street
London SW18 4JJ

ISBN 0 232 52614 1

A catalogue record for this book is available from the British Library.

Designed and produced by Sandie Boccacci
Phototypeset in 11/14pt Minion
Printed and bound in Great Britain by
Page Bros, Norwich, Norfolk

Contents

Acknowledgements   vii

Foreword by the Dean of St Paul's   ix

Introduction   1

1. How Should the World Be Governed?   11

2. Is There an Alternative to Global Capitalism?   43

3. Environment and Humanity: Friends or Foes?   71

4. Is Humanity Killing Itself?   97

Afterword by the Archbishop of Canterbury   125

Acknowledgements

We are deeply grateful to all our colleagues at St Paul's Cathedral who helped in so many ways to bring *The Worlds We Live In* to fruition. In particular, the organisation of the whole series was overseen with great professionalism and good humour by Elizabeth Foy, the Manager of St Paul's Institute. We also wish to thank Clare McCaldin, who was closely involved in the early stages of planning, Anya Matthews and Mark McVay for their assistance with media coverage, Kim Kendall for her administrative assistance and hospitality, and Sabina Alkire for helping to shape the series. *The Worlds We Live In* was planned in close collaboration with staff from Lambeth Palace, and we thank Jonathan Jennings and Jeremy Harris in particular for their involvement with the project. Amongst others who have contributed, Rupert Shreeve designed the poster and leaflets for the series and the image used on the cover of this book. The dialogues were recorded by R. G. Jones, who also came to the rescue to overcome problems with the sound system.

We are indebted to Elizabeth Foy and Carol Bollard for transcribing the texts of the dialogues, which made our job as editors much easier, to Virginia Hearn at Darton, Longman and Todd for overseeing the production of this book with care and enthusiasm, and to Susan Newell, who not only brought the youngest member of the audience (aged three months) to every dialogue but assisted with the editing.

Our thanks go most of all to those who participated in the dialogues: to Mark Tully, Shirley Williams, Lucy Winkett and Elizabeth Butler-Sloss for chairing each event with great professionalism and sensitivity; to the interlocutors, David Owen, Philip Bobbitt, Muhammad Yunus, John Kay, Mary Midgley, Ricardo Navarro, Ian Smith and Peter Bains for their willingness to share their wealth of expertise and insights in the discussions; and especially to Rowan Williams, who not only took on a daunting intellectual challenge and a major commitment in a busy schedule, but did so with great enthusiasm.

Both the organisers and the participants wish to thank all who attended and contributed to making *The Worlds We Live In* a memorable and worthwhile series.

Claire Foster and Edmund Newell

Foreword

There is a memorial tablet set in the ground in the north-eastern corner of the Churchyard of St Paul's Cathedral which simply reads, 'Here stood Paul's Cross'. For three or four hundred years, it was to Paul's Cross that people came in large numbers from all over London for proclamations, sermons and public disputations.

The memorial tablet serves to remind us that there is a continuing responsibility to ensure that our Cathedrals are places of dialogue and debate. I have no doubt that they have unique opportunities for bringing into the forefront of public discourse some of the large questions with which we are all wrestling.

This is the conviction that underscores the work of the newly established St Paul's Institute. It is concerned – in partnership with others in the City of London and elsewhere – to explore questions concerning global finance, ethics and public values. But these topics raise questions about the sort of world in which we live today, and what we are doing to ourselves as a species, and what sort of world we want to pass on to our children.

It has therefore been very good to welcome the Archbishop of Canterbury to St Paul's for a series of dialogues in which he is able to explore with others *The Worlds We Live In*. I write on behalf of all my Chapter colleagues at St Paul's to acknowledge our indebtedness to the Director and the Deputy Director of the Institute and to all who have assisted us in this venture. I hope this book will enable many who could not be with us at St Paul's to share in the discussion.

John Moses, Dean of St Paul's

Introduction

It was always envisaged that the newly founded St Paul's Institute at St Paul's Cathedral would offer a public space for debate and dialogue on contemporary issues. It was also intended that the Institute would make room for the ethical and spiritual dimensions of those issues. The series entitled *The Worlds We Live In*, of which this book is the record, attempted to fulfil both those aims.

The internal space of St Paul's is dominated and defined by a dome that is known the world over. The dome can be seen as symbolising the ideals of holism, unity, connectedness, inter-relationship – as an all-embracing space that puts Wisdom and true perception before power and mightiness.

St Paul's is also a huge building. It can seat some two and a half thousand people and has the benefit of being well known. It can therefore offer a platform for public engagement that is rivalled by few other places. And because it is above all a spiritual place, it ensures that any public – or indeed private – conversation that happens there is felt to be divinely witnessed. This has some curious effects. Lecturers have remarked on how the building influences what they say and how they say it. Celebrity figures speaking of global concerns lose their iconic status, as the focus – without anyone doing anything to make this happen – shifts from the *person* to the *issue* being offered for consideration in the presence of God. That same presence, while diminishing celebrity status, confers equality of status on all present. In the presence of God, everyone in the building is afforded the same respect and tolerance.

We sought to magnify this natural equity by making the dialogues accessible. The posters (similar to the cover of this book) were in a contemporary style, designed by a student to attract unchurched eyes. The events were free at the point of entry (though the cost of staging such events – not least getting the acoustics right – necessitated having retiring collections). The people who came were diverse. Three young men at the first dialogue, who were slipping away half an hour before the end, told us they had dropped in because it looked interesting, but they had to get away for the football. They assured us they were not leaving because the dialogue was boring.

The choice of the title of the series reflects a sense that people can and do live in different worlds, shaped by their perception, their education and training, their beliefs and their prejudices. It also acknowledges that the realms of governance, economics, ecology and health are in some senses distinct and evoke different disciplines and approaches. However, the same Archbishop participating in all four dialogues was an outward, symbolic demonstration of the fact that these apparently different worlds are inextricably linked. Like a *sutra*, a golden thread, the Archbishop joined each dialogue to the next one and showed that, in fact, there really is only one world and that the four areas under discussion simply cannot be addressed in isolation from one another.

The Archbishop also presented an exemplary display of specifically Christian engagement with contemporary issues. He invited dialogue partners who brought very different perspectives to the subjects under discussion, and he first of all *listened* to them. Then he responded, indicating his own understanding of each of the issues, which was not inconsiderable, but at the same time challenging his interlocutors to take what they thought about the issues much, much deeper. How can international politics unite diverse people made in God's image? How can global economics enable human flourishing? What is the natural world telling us of God's communication with us? Is there a division between physical health and spiritual well-being? The effect of the Archbishop's probing was that the audience, who were given the opportunity to submit written questions to the panel, were left not only with a better understanding of the issues, but also with a more profound engagement with them.

It was a characteristic of the series that the interlocutors were not chosen for having diametrically opposing views to each other or to the Archbishop, but rather that they brought varied perspectives and experience to the discussion. We did not see heated rows. We did not witness arguments where the audience were asked to choose one solution as against another. Week by week we saw three extremely polite people, chaired by equally polite facilitators, sharing their perspectives and evolving a richer elucidation of the subjects thereby. Everyone was being educated.

The first dialogue, 'How Should the World Be Governed?', tackled the extremely complex but important issue of how people throughout the world can work co-operatively in the political sphere. As globalisation breaks down the traditional barriers between countries and regions, and as so many important issues – not least security and care of the environment – require international solutions, the political scene is becoming increasingly globalised. The extensive media coverage of and intense public interest in the US presidential elections of 2004 highlights this, because of the recognition that the election of the President of the world's only current superpower has implications that spread well beyond the borders of the United States. Similarly, the profile of the United Nations has increased significantly in recent years. In the run-up to the last Iraq war, the focus of the world was on the United Nations and its Security Council. The way events played out then and subsequently has only intensified concerns about how collective international decisions are made and actions taken.

This dialogue brought together a wide range of experience and perspectives on international politics through its participants. It was chaired by the distinguished broadcaster Sir Mark Tully, who as well as being an expert on India and South-East Asia, lives and works for much of the time in New Delhi. Lord Owen, as well as being Foreign Secretary (1977–79), was the European Union negotiator during the Balkans conflict and was the Co-Chair of the International Conference for the Former Yugoslavia. In this respect, he has been deeply involved in some of the most difficult aspects of international politics, dealing with international military and diplomatic co-operation on the one hand, and the more localised divisions between neighbouring countries, cultures and ethnic groups on the other. As someone who has worked in and with international political structures and brokered deals in the international arena, it is interesting to hear his affirmation of those structures as being fundamentally sound and fit for the challenges of the twenty-first century. More important for him is the need for compromise and collaboration between nations in working for the common good.

The role of the nation state is an important part of the dialogue. Professor Philip Bobbitt is no stranger to the world of practical politics, having worked in the White House and the State Department, as well as holding a Chair in Law at the University of Texas. From his perspective, however, he sees the erosion of the nation state, which is being replaced by what he terms the 'market state', where market forces are increasingly playing their part in driving international politics. While not championing this change, he sees the need for existing institutions to acknowledge and respond to the pressure of market forces.

Although this is not explored explicitly in the dialogue, the Archbishop, as head of the Anglican Communion, also brings into the discussion his own insights on international relations – not least at a time of tension and division within the Communion. Perhaps the discussion on the role and purpose of formal structures, and the influence of other forces in the international arena, resonates with his own experiences with the Anglican Communion and its constituent churches. Within the discussion, the Archbishop highlights the role that NGOs, civil society groups and faith communities can play in the changing world of international politics, contributing within existing structures but recognising that new ways of operating offer fresh opportunities for people of faith and goodwill to work to shape the world in which we live.

The discussion prompted a wide range of questions from the floor which, amongst other things, led to discussion on the role of the Internet in global politics, the composition of the UN Security Council, the way the United States exercises its power and influence, and, not surprisingly, whether religion is a cause of or a solution to international conflict.

The first dialogue provides the backdrop for the rest of the series, for tackling the challenges of global economics, the environment and public health requires a workable political framework that promotes a global worldview and allows for international co-operation. The importance of institutional structures is highlighted in the second dialogue, 'Is There an Alternative to Global Capitalism?' chaired by Baroness Shirley Williams. Much of the discussion revolves around making markets work effectively and fairly. Muhammad Yunus, the founder of the Grameen Bank in Bangladesh, which has pioneered micro-credit with great success, regards many of the institutional structures in finance and economics as biased against the poor and in need of reform. His plea is to create economic structures which would support the expansion of social enterprise, where the objective of the business activity is to do good for society at large and in particular to empower the poor to lift themselves out of poverty through their own enterprise. John Kay, one of Britain's most distinguished economists, also focuses on the importance of economic activity being embedded in stable political and social structures. He is optimistic about the potential for capitalism as it is currently practised to deliver benefits to society as a whole, so long as the checks and balances provided by these structures are in place.

The Archbishop, who has seen at first hand the effect of micro-credit through the establishment of credit unions in Wales, is also keen to explore the potential of social entrepreneurship. His particular concern over the way global capitalism is currently practised is that the fluidity of money enables capital to move in and out of economies at will, irrespective of the social consequences of rapid investment and disinvestment. His emphasis is on finding ways of embedding economic development within societies for the good of all. Social enterprise offers a more stable, long-term means for economic development amongst the poor. The Archbishop also looks at what role the churches might play in the economic sphere following their influential role in the Jubilee 2000 movement for the alleviation of international debt in developing countries.

Questions from the floor covered topics including the role of the market economy in promoting development, the viability of the proposed Tobin Tax, whether economic growth is sustainable, and the relationship between micro-credit and commercial banking.

The third dialogue, 'Environment and Humanity – Friends or Foes?', chaired by Canon Lucy Winkett, explores the relationship between human beings and the rest of the planet. The title reflects the growing sense, echoed in the writings of many commentators, that the human species has wittingly or unwittingly taken on a kind of rogue status. Not least by the discovery of penicillin, one of the great achievements of the twentieth century, humans have managed to gain the edge over other species, which now have to manoeuvre themselves with increasing agility around human beings and habitats. Only those that are useful to humans or can adapt to human habitats are, it seems, guaranteed survival. But as we all know, the loss of species precipitates the loss of biological diversity, on which every living thing depends. The writer E. O. Wilson thinks we are heading for the 'eremezoic era' – the era of loneliness, in which humans have so poisoned the world around them that they have to create an artificial world in which they can survive.[1]

1. E. O. Wilson, *The diversity of life* (London, Penguin Books, 2001).

Christianity has played its part in this negative process by allowing human beings to believe that, God having special purposes for them, they can exploit the natural world to their own, God-given (as they believed) ends, justified by the dominion that Genesis 1:26 conferred on them. Now there is a growing understanding of the profound interconnectedness of all things, the shared evolutionary history that, once known, removes any notion of humans living as tenants on the face of the planet and places us fairly and squarely as co-participants in the glorious, seemingly infinite diversity on earth. In this dialogue, Dr Midgely, academic and author, argues very strongly for this perception, using the mythology of the Gaia concept to show what she means. She says that the idea of Gaia is an excellent one for dislodging the mechanistic, atomistic view of the universe and ourselves that permits exploitation. It is our images, our imaginations, of ourselves as isolated from a world that is made of inert matter, that create the situation in which we can do so much harm to the environment. The Archbishop compares her Gaia concept with that of Wisdom, which permeates all things as their true integrity and creativity, inextricably joining everything to everything else.

Dr Navarro, Chair of Friends of the Earth International (until 2004) and an activist in his home country of El Salvador, has startling evidence of the consequences of human exploitation. The treatment of humans cannot be separated, he argues, from the way the planet is treated. He insists that in the absence of political will, the changes in behaviour that the planet so desperately needs cannot happen. Sustainable development, commonly understood as evolving economic, environmental and social well-being, is meaningless without the addition of political well-being. This translates in practice into communities genuinely taking ownership of decisions that affect them.

The questions from the floor are excellent, raising issues such as what the churches can do; the value of small-scale projects in the face of a vast problem; the implications of the Christian concept of stewardship; the use of the imagination and the effect of becoming a largely urban species on our imaginations; and the merits or otherwise of nuclear power.

The Archbishop ends the dialogue by calling for a new asceticism: 'Go for a walk. Get wet. Dig the earth.' In such simple and direct ways people can re-engage with the natural world, and thereby open the way to re-engaging with themselves as spiritual beings but also as politically engaged beings.

The concluding dialogue on health, chaired by Dame Elizabeth Butler-Sloss, is entitled 'Is Humanity Killing Itself?' in recognition of two disturbing contemporary observations. One is that, following a 50-year pharmaceutical honeymoon during which we could begin to believe that there was a pill to cure everything, new diseases, or variants of old ones, are emerging that no pill can treat. The other observation is that, while it is still true that most Westerners can enjoy reasonable health and access to high-technology health care, two thirds of the world have no such access. Conditions that are eminently treatable are killing millions of people around the globe, every day.

The two interlocutors for this dialogue are from the fields of public and private health. Dr Ian Smith worked for many years as a medical missionary in Nepal, then latterly as an adviser to the Director General of the World Health Organisation (WHO). Mr Peter Bains is Senior Vice-President of the international arm of Glaxo SmithKline, the largest multinational pharmaceutical company in the world. In their introductions to the dialogue, both interlocutors use the same statistics to demonstrate that the answer to the question 'Is Humanity Killing Itself?' hangs, rather terrifyingly, in the balance. Both are able to provide breakdowns of headline statistics that paint horrifying pictures, almost always focusing on Africa. The average longevity of humans has gone up overall, but in parts of Africa it has fallen drastically. For example, life expectancy in Japan is now at 85 years, while in Sierra Leone it is a mere 36 years. Childhood deaths show a global improvement, but whereas in Finland and Iceland childhood mortality is 4 per cent, in Sierra Leone it is 30 per cent.

It is a heartening feature of this dialogue, given the daily tragedies, that there is demonstrably a fresh willingness for the public and private spheres to work in partnership. Where health care is genuinely being improved, this is happening because of serious efforts to pool the different skills available from different sources. Research and development, funded by the pharmaceutical industry (through profits made from patented medicines), can and sometimes do come together with local efforts to provide accessible health clinics and adequately trained personnel to staff them. It is clear from the discussion, however, that these success stories are few and far between, and only work when the wider political context is sufficiently supportive – or sufficiently distant. Without political will in the countries where access to medicines is needed, no real change will be seen.

The Archbishop links health with the exercise of real democracy. He sees the ability of people to participate in the decisions that affect their lives as key to their good health. This again emphasises the obstacle that an obstructive or corrupt political system can be to the creation of healthy communities.

The Archbishop also probes the dimension of spiritual health, suggesting that good health can be seen as an attunement to the world at large. This links it inextricably to the ecological and political dimensions of people's lives. He speaks of the body as a good gift of God to be treasured and nurtured and, therefore, accorded the deepest possible respect.

The audience interrogates the dialogue group with questions such as whether over-population is by itself a threat to human health, or whether the greater threat is the West's over-consumption: 'Why are two thirds of the world hungry when the other one third is trying to lose weight?' There are questions about the disbenefits of intellectual property rights and the use of animals in medical research. The question time ends with a surprising answer from the Archbishop to the question, 'Is faith good for your health?'

The dialogue series *The Worlds We Live In* was not intended to be a platform for the Archbishop of Canterbury to tell a waiting world his views on every issue under the sun. It was created to allow him to fulfil one of the most important tasks of any religious leader: to reach into the deepest core of his faith, in this case Christianity, and to bring forth spiritual fruits that are both ancient and also entirely fresh and new, into the heart of the material concerns of our world, for the sake of the world. The transcripts of the dialogues that follow in the pages of this book, edited as lightly as possible to retain the sense and feel of a live and spontaneous discussion, demonstrate that Dr Williams succeeded in this difficult task.

Claire Foster and Edmund Newell

Chapter One
How Should the World Be Governed?

The first St Paul's Institute dialogue was held at St Paul's Cathedral on 8 September 2004 between Dr Rowan Williams, Archbishop of Canterbury, Professor Philip Bobbitt and Lord David Owen. It was chaired by Sir Mark Tully, one of Britain's most distinguished broadcasters. For 22 years he was the BBC's India and South-East Asia correspondent.

Sir Mark Tully: Good evening. I have been told very strictly that I do not have to present a paper, so I do not want to say anything more beyond reminding you that the subject is 'How Should the World be Governed?' It seems to me one of the subjects which will come up is roles: What role should the United Nations play? What role should nation states play? What role should regional groupings play? What role should NGOs and faith communities play? What role should multinational corporations play? And finally, and of course very importantly, what role should individuals play? The form that these dialogues will take will be that each speaker will make a short presentation, then we will have dialogue, and then we will have questions.

Now it is my immense privilege to introduce the participants in the dialogue. Dr Rowan Williams is the 104th Archbishop of Canterbury, and in this role he has established himself as a distinguished commentator on the issues of the day. Previously he was Archbishop of Wales and Bishop of Monmouth, and Lady Margaret Professor of Divinity at Oxford University. He is the author of numerous books on theology and spirituality, as well as two volumes of poetry. On his move from Monmouth to Canterbury, the First Minister of Wales, Rhodri Morgan, said of him, 'Rowan Williams is a man in a million and people of his calibre come along only every 200–300 years.'

Lord Owen was Foreign Secretary from 1977 to 1979. He was one of the founders of the SDP and its leader for four years. He was European Union negotiator during the Balkans conflict and co-chair of the International Conference for the Former Yugoslavia. He now sits in the House of Lords as a cross-bench Peer.

Philip Bobbitt is a historian of nuclear strategy and Professor of Law at the University of Texas. He's served in the White House, the State Department and on the National Security Council, and is perhaps best known for his book, *The Shield of Achilles: War, Peace and the Course of History*.

I will now ask Lord Owen to make his statement.

Lord Owen: I am reasonably optimistic about the government of the world. That may come as a surprise to many of you living in the shadow still of September 11th. It is easy to think that the world is a worse place and the government of the world is worse now. But I do think we need to remember that we have lived in a century with two world wars, both starting in Europe, and a long and, in my judgement, extremely dangerous Cold War where at various stages we got quite close to blowing our world up, or a very substantial part of it. And since the fall of the Berlin Wall we have begun to see the Security Council of the United Nations functioning as some hoped it might function when it was created in San Francisco in 1945. At least there was not a total stand-off, at least the Russian Federation has come into the dialogue, and China has come much more into the dialogue in the Security Council. Of course we live in the shadow of the major and very well-known disagreements over Iraq, but at least they were argued out in the Security Council. Different positions were taken but the world heard the different voices and there was not, in my view, a sufficient mood of compromise – possibly and arguably not a sufficient mood of compromise even within the European Union – but the structure seemed to be there.

What is necessary is a greater commitment of sovereign nations to work together and to reach compromises and to seek out a genuine consensus wherever they can. What are the best hopes? First and foremost, it seems to me the Security Council has to discipline itself more and be ready to take difficult decisions, and then answer for them and not blame the UN and not use the UN as a scapegoat, which has been the familiar pattern in the past.

I think it is also essential that we start to function more effectively in all the different specialised agencies for world governance. As I am a doctor, I suppose I start with the World Health Organisation. We should not forget that we have eradicated smallpox, and we have made very big advances on some of the global illnesses. Leprosy is still with us, tragically, tuberculosis has come back, but there is a formidable record of achievement in public health. If we look at the other agencies, the economic agencies often called the Bretton Woods system, we have not made as big a progress as I think many of us would have wished. But even so, we have more choice, the market system operates, the World Trade Organisation is trying to remove protectionist barriers. We are not making anywhere near enough progress, but the structures are there and they have begun to gel together in some respects. We can also highlight the cultural activities of UNESCO.[1] Also, the increased

1. United Nations Education, Scientific and Cultural Organisation.

role of women in government has been a dramatic change for the better over the years, helped in some part by the United Nations. Certainly we have seen a world in which the place of women has been far more established, far more influential.

I know we need to do more about stopping wars. I know sometimes church people feel there is no place for war. However, there have been reputable arguments for just wars, and I think there is also a need to understand that force is necessary at times for keeping the peace. There is also this whole new area of humanitarian interventions in sovereign states, which used to be completely *verboten*. Basically, the interpretation of the UN Charter meant that in all the Cold War years there was no possibility of any intervention in a sovereign state. That's changed. We have intervened, often for the best of intentions. But some of our interventions have had very bad consequences. So when I look forward – and we will discuss the various optimistic, and perhaps pessimistic scenarios – I think the chances of our being better governed in thirty years' time are pretty strong. Thank you.

Sir Mark Tully: Now I would ask Professor Bobbitt to make his presentation.

Professor Bobbitt: How should the world be governed? This is a rather large question when, as Woody Allen reminds, us, 'It is hard enough to find your way around Brooklyn.' But in this place and in these auspices I am going to give it a try.

The UN Charter is the basic constitutional framework for the society of nation states. This constitution, having achieved so much, is unravelling as *ad hoc* arrangements like those that fought the war in Kosovo and the recent coalition that invaded Iraq marginalise the role of the international institutions of the society of nation states. Some blame the United States for this as the world's most powerful state, which seems to have turned its back on the very institutions for which it fought. Some blame other states that have paralysed the Security Council in Yugoslavia, Rwanda, Iraq and the Near East, and rendered its resolutions practically unenforceable save by unilateral action.

The real thought is simply that organisations made out of nation states are not very good at dealing with transnational crises and threats of the present: SARS and AIDS, the proliferation of nuclear weapons, global terrorism, climate change, and humanitarian crises. The reason we are unable to get a UN resolution on Darfur this week, for example, is because the Russians will veto it to protect their economic interests in Sudan. One could tell similar stories about the Americans, the French, and even the British.

For this and other reasons, the nation state is being superseded by a new constitutional order that will resemble that of the twenty-first-century multinational corporation, with its global interests, more than the twentieth-century state. It will out-source many functions to the private sector, rely less on war and regulation and more on market incentives. It will respond to ever-changing consumer demand rather than to voter preferences expressed in relatively rare elections.

This new constitutional order, which I will call the 'market state', has not arrived, but one can already see evidence of its approach. From the perspective of nation states, to which we are all accustomed, market states seem to be a disavowal of everything we have been taught to expect from the state. With regard to global governance, this may seem like a renunciation of the rule of law itself. Many members of the fraternity of international lawyers have set themselves the task of defending our current arrangements as if this, rather than solving the problems our institutions were set up to treat, were the duty of those who want to preserve the rule of law in a period of deep and fundamental change.

In much of Europe we see a preference for law to the exclusion of strategy. American action against Iraq is deplored, but no one told us exactly how Saddam Hussein was to be brought into obedience within the norms of human rights and his international undertakings. In America we see a preference for strategy to the exclusion of law. We are told that force must be used to pre-empt potentially mortal threats. But we are not told what standards permit US action against Iraq but do not favour Indian action against Pakistan, North Korean action against South Korea, Iranian action against Israel, or vice versa for that matter.

Unlike nation states, market states unite law and strategy. Indeed, we face threats like global terrorism and the need for humanitarian intervention, that cannot be met without a broad-based sense among the world's publics that the use of force is legitimate. What will establish the legitimacy of a society of market states in the eyes of the world? My guess is that it will be the market state's unique ability to partner with non-state organisations, as well as its global perspective. Global governance that emerges from a decentralised, out-sourcing, market-orientated network of states will allow for a number of different non-state institutions to work together for the global good. NGOs (non-governmental organisations), multinational corporations, UN agencies like the WHO, and the media can all provide potential partners for global governance.

International NGOs do not have a basis in legitimacy that is provided by a democratic process. But it is worse than idle to propose a global role for a universal democracy, giving the most populous states decisive authority in determining global policies for a world parliament. This would assume that because democracy is legitimating for individual state governance, it is the only legitimating method for global governance. But there is no global state. Indeed, global governance does not entail a global government. The market state shifts the domestic focus from groups to the individual.

A related objective must prevail in the international arena. The structures of global governance in this century must be based on the primacy of individuals as members of self-chosen and overlapping groups, rather than the primacy of nations or nation states. When a new society of states emerges we will find that it too has a constitution. Our duty is to see that it is a humane one, that it gives privilege to the health, safety and opportunity of the peoples of this earth, and not to nation states that generally do not have the common interest sufficient to address global problems. Paradoxically, perhaps this means that we live in a period of great opportunity.

Sir Mark Tully: Thank you very much. Now I will ask the Archbishop to make his initial response, and then we will open the discussion.

Archbishop: Professor Bobbitt used the word 'transnational' at one point, and I think this is key to understanding the agenda we are trying to address tonight.

Internationalism is about how nation states negotiate with each other as if they were themselves individuals. And, as has been said, many of our assumptions about the governance of the world at the moment rest on the model of the individual sovereign state – a self-contained unit with an unchallengeable supreme legal authority which then negotiates with others under the umbrella of something like the United Nations Charter. Lord Owen is right that the United Nations Charter is not a dead letter, and the achievements that have developed under its auspices are serious. But if we begin to enumerate the kinds of problem in our world that can never be resolved by the negotiation of individual sovereign states, we see that there is a serious challenge, not just about how well our present institutions work but about the assumptions upon which they work.

Many people these days talk about global civil society. We know roughly what institutions of civil society are about in our own context. They are those non-governmental, concern-focused groups which, outside the statutory patterns of public life, maintain certain concerns and interests about how human

beings live together. They may have to do with the good order-
ing of communities, with the rights and opportunities of
women and the protection of children – though those are
statutory matters as well. They may have to do with consumer
pressure and capacity building. But the nature of the challenges
that we face across national boundaries is such that we need to
think of a global role for civil society institutions.

We have been reminded that the economic developments of
the last couple of decades and the globalisation of the world's
economy mean that no one state can fully determine its own
economic destiny. Issues around refugees and displaced persons
and their rights once again make it difficult simply to think in
terms of sovereign states as self-contained units. And the whole
cluster of issues around how we build capacity in impover-
ished, disadvantaged communities, and how we address global
health issues in an age of unprecedented mobility, once again
questions the sovereignty model with which we have been
working.

The challenge that has been put before us, and which I hope
we will now discuss further, is not only how the institutions
around the United Nations and its Charter can be made to
function more effectively; it is also about how those institutions
open themselves up to the contribution of institutions of global
civil society: how NGOs and similar groups have a voice that is
audible in the international institutions we have. I don't mean,
as some people have occasionally suggested, that NGOs and
civil society organisations should have a role as of right in the
UN Security Council. How an institution like the Security
Council registers and responds to the issues that are covered by
such groups is a fair question, and I would see in the middle
distance perhaps two developments which are worth pursuing
and exploring. One is a re-thinking of the workings of the
Security Council that would give certain groups a right of
audience. The second is the development not only of regional
groups of nations looking at issues around security, but other

kinds of alliance of groups of nations, with common democratic commitments, common understandings of human rights.

Finally, if we are looking to a future dominated neither by some sort of world government, nor by a clinging on to the existing pattern of negotiations between nation states, we need, I believe, to think very seriously about how the voice of global civil society is heard. Looking at the issues of health, capacity building, environmental care and concern, the welfare of women and children, we must consider how these groups can have audience and how local and issue-focused coalitions of nations can work together for the sake of security and common moral vision.

Sir Mark Tully: Lord Owen, you were the most optimistic about the present situation. How do you respond to the Archbishop's suggestions of changes which need to be made?

Lord Owen: Well, I question this erosion of the sovereign nation. I think that you can easily exaggerate this. The problem for the world was, and still remains, that too many countries are not democratic. I think civil-society groups, NGOs and focus-interest groups have a big role to play in an ongoing democracy. But we have to face it that it is extremely difficult for them to have any effect if there is no democratic base for them to work on. That is why we have to organise ourselves in nation states.

The nation state seems to be what people can identify with, and I think that a system of governance has got to be one in which people can identify with the decision-making. I am personally a great de-centralist. We have to face the fact that the biggest country in the world, China, is neither a democratic country and nor would its leaders want it to be a democratic country. And there are many other countries that are run by dictators, or people who may aspire to democratic principles but don't follow them. So by all means encourage alternatives. We in this country are participating in an alternative, which is the European Union. The EU is very tentative, yet there is a tendency at the moment to feel that it is more than it is, to talk about it as if it is a state – Professor Bobbitt has used the word, 'an umbrella state'. But the EU is a long way from being a state, and its members are a long way from agreeing on many issues. We could not agree on Iraq, we could not agree on economic policy, we cannot agree on whether or not to have a single currency. This doesn't surprise me. The EU will take decades to evolve. The EU is, in my view, a great idealistic venture, that can't be driven too fast and has to go at a pace which people understand and people can relate to.

I think that this break-up of the sovereign nations is not going to happen as fast as either of my fellow discussants seem to think. Nor do I think it is desirable. I find it hard to believe that there are many issues which we cannot, given the will and the commitment, negotiate amongst ourselves as sovereign nations and reach global solutions, because most of those global solutions are actually in our own self-interest. One of the reasons why the Kyoto Treaty was not agreed to was that it was not seen by some of the key non-signatories, such as the United States and Russia, as being sufficiently in their interest. Ninety-six US Senators voted against the Kyoto Treaty. I think that is one of the problems. You can aspire at a bureaucratic international level to a solution, but if you cannot carry your own people with you, then it won't stand up even if you have reached agreement.

Sir Mark Tully: Would you like to speak, Archbishop?

Archbishop: I am not at all questioning the significance of the role of democracy, nor of the accessibility of democratic institutions, which I think is the point that is most important here. Indeed, the building of civil society is, as Lord Owen has indicated, a crucial element in the evolution of a mature democracy.

I should clarify two different points which I may have pushed together too much in my initial remarks. The first is that I am less sanguine about the integrity of the nation state simply because of the globalisation of our economic life, which has already made more porous in all sorts of ways the boundaries that were once taken for granted. I would also say that any effective solution to some of the transnational challenges we face is going to involve a redefinition of sovereignty – what one writer called a pooling of sovereignty – between sovereign states rather than just the negotiation of interests. Of course, no existing government can undertake this without democratic consent, but I think it's increasingly urgent that the nettle be grasped of effective transnational agreements, which may appear to cede elements of sovereignty as it has been understood.

Sir Mark Tully: Professor Bobbitt, you were the one who took the most pessimistic view of the condition of the nation state.

Professor Bobbitt: The most pessimistic view of the nation state, but the most optimistic view of the future and what can be done with it.

When I came to study in the UK in 1981, one of the movements in this country, as in mine, which people like David Owen – whom I so greatly admired – were a part of, was trying to balance citizens' rights with responsibilities. We had gotten the idea that a citizen who has only rights, who only asserts rights against other citizens, misses half of the equation. Something about our rights lies inexplicably connected with our responsibilities to others. That has happened in the civil societies of many states now, and I think we are all aware of this right across party lines.

It is also happening now among states. For a very long time a kind of opaque sovereignty shielded states so that whatever they did within their borders – however they mistreated their citizens, whatever authority they used to justify their rule, whatever weapons they wished to acquire – was really a matter of their own business. After all, it was their society. Sovereignty was something their state inherited.

I think fewer and fewer people believe this now. They think that sovereignty has something to do not just with rights, but also with responsibilities. Some people believe in a kind of translucent sovereignty, that sovereignty comes from the collective institutional judgements of states, so that the United Nations, for example, can qualify the sovereignty of the state as it did with respect to the no-fly zones in Iraq.

Some people believe in a transparent sovereignty – sovereignty that doesn't descend from above but actually arises from the people. If you are a society of fair and just and democratic institutions, your sovereignty is as solid as it can be, though you may wish to trade in it the way societies have in Europe who created a market in sovereignty. If, on the other hand, you brutalise your own people with campaigns of genocide or ethnic cleansing, your government cannot defend itself on the basis of its sovereignty because it has stripped itself, it has qualified and compromised its own sovereignty, by the way it has treated its people or its neighbours.

David Owen remarks that the structures we have now are really all right. What is needed is more will and more commitment on the part of the participants. I spend a lot of my life around the participants and, I must say, although they may not all be of the calibre of Lord Owen, they are of a very high calibre indeed, and yet that has not helped us. International institutions clustered around Bosnia, but none of them was able to stop the carnage. International institutions are ever present in the Israel–Palestine conflict, but how much closer have they, despite the best will, been able to bring us to a just peace for both those peoples? I think the answer probably does lie in the structures, and I am quite confident that these structures are undergoing immense change.

Sir Mark Tully: Archbishop, would you like to follow up on this question of rights and responsibilities? It does seem to me that we do need to write responsibility into our global, national and individual life, and that we hear almost only of rights.

Archbishop: I am very grateful to Professor Bobbitt for what he said about sovereignty in relation to responsibility as well as rights. The way we have used the term 'sovereignty' has often been as a kind of protective device, rather than something which is positive, something which can be taken into a pattern of common action with common aspiration. And we haven't always thought very seriously about the circumstances in which sovereignty is compromised or even forfeited.

The nation state as it's evolved – as that phrase makes clear – has a history, and the concept of the sovereign nation state as expressed in the United Nations Charter is not one that simply drops from heaven. That means that we will always be at least in some way capable of thinking through issues of why sovereignty is legitimate, so there are moral and legal questions around which enshrine these issues about responsibility. So I warm very much to that.

I think that what Lord Owen has been saying about the capacity of sovereign states to work together effectively because of their recognition of long-term self-interest is plausible up to a point. My concern is how there is any form of arbitration of national interest, or even group national interest. I don't really know the answer to that, but I am looking, I suppose, to a re-vitalised United Nations structure to provide some space in which those issues about legitimacy and the right exercise of responsibility can at least be raised.

Lord Owen: One of the interesting things in the United States is that despite having Presidents – particularly the present one, but it is not unique to him – and a Congress that seem to think that they can be hostile to, disparaging of, or even write off, the

United Nations, poll after poll shows that United States citizens have a very high level of commitment to the United Nations.

I think there is this juxtaposition in other countries as well. We have had an aspiration to have 0.77 per cent of our GDP devoted to overseas aid. I can only remember one Election – I think it was the first Election in 1974 – when the churches managed to build up a campaign so that you couldn't fight that General Election without being asked about your commitment to the aid target. It really seemed for a while that votes were involved. Our aid targets have not been met, and people keep promising but they don't keep to it.

This is where the special-interest groups can mobilise and make the politicians face up to the argument of self-interest. We do have a very active overseas charities movement in this country. There is a public response to national disasters which actually comes in hard pounds contributed. So there is out there, it seems to me, a more responsible electorate than has yet been reflected in the decisions in Parliament.

Also, when we talk about the sovereign states, let's remember they do finance the World Bank, they finance the IMF, they finance WHO, they finance UNESCO. Now again, very often these organisations are pretty tight for resources. I can remember as Minister of Health being asked by the officials who were very committed to the smallpox eradication programme what they could do, because the programme in Ethiopia was running out of money. The Swedish government gave a million and we gave a million and the programme kept going.

Mobilising the political system seems to me to be one of the most important areas, together with focused activity and pressure. The institutions didn't fail Bosnia. The fact was – and I was very close to it – that none of those heads of government was prepared to commit troops on the ground in a way in which they would actually fight the Serbs. That was a reality. Not until after Srebrenica was the American President ready to put troops in, and then immediately the Europeans were ready

to do so. And so you come back to people – much more important, I think, than institutions.

I do not believe we would have had the fall of the Berlin Wall
had there not been an understanding growing on the whole
issue of *détente* between East and West. If you are on the right
of politics, you could say *détente* was due to Mrs Thatcher and
President Reagan jacking up the arms building, pressurising
the Soviet Union. If you are on the left, you would tend to say
it was due to a long process of *détente*, often scoffed at by the
right, that was started by Willy Brandt. Actually I think both of
these factors, and many others besides, contributed. But at the
crucial moment we needed a relationship between President
Bush Senior and Chancellor Kohl in Germany. The Americans
wanted the reunification of Germany. The French President
and the British Prime Minister at the time were highly scepti-
cal about it. And then you needed the almost incoherence of
Gorbachev, who was not ready to use force to impose the
settlement and also wanted to have a dialogue going with both
Kohl and with Bush. Now for all the amount we write in
academic papers, it's my experience, time after time, that
major decisions of the world are determined by the juxta-
positions of key individuals who are prepared to take certain
decisions for good or ill.

Professor Bobbitt: That has also been my experience. But I would
say that it really is false to separate people from institutions.
There are no civilised persons who do their jobs, relate to other
people, raise their families, educate students, fight wars, without some institutional structure within which they act. So I
don't think its people *or* structures necessarily. Instead, I think
we now have very dedicated, thoughtful and able persons
standing at an unusual moment in the change of our institutions. We are not bringing it about, but it is being brought
about. They can resist it but it will come. The most creative of
these leaders will be able to operate both in the old system and

in the new. But I don't think that simply saying they should just be better is going to help them or us.

Archbishop: I wonder if I could come back on the question of a public with a higher moral vision than we sometimes assume. There have been two things in recent years which have given a strong illustration of this. One, which I mention because it was very close to my heart and a priority at the time, was the Jubilee 2000 campaign, in which largely the churches brought very heavy pressure to bear on our government on the question of the remission of international debt. I was at the memorable event in Birmingham, where some 70,000 people had gathered, when we heard that representatives of our own government had taken note of precisely what we were talking and protesting about, and were willing to meet and talk face to face in a way which I don't think we'd expected. There has also been the development in the last couple of decades of consumer pressure applied to the methods and standards of multinational organisations and corporations.

I think both of these instances are very positive, but I would add a caveat here and go back to something I was saying earlier. When the Jubilee 2000 campaign ended, many people asked, 'What do we do next? Where is the next focus?' Among the urgent issues that were raised that have led to further coalitions developing was a cluster of questions around trade justice, the impacting of intellectual property rights agreements on bio-forms in disadvantaged countries, and so forth. One of the problems of that second wave borne from the Jubilee 2000 experience was that whereas Jubilee 2000 could address itself fairly directly to our government, with many of the issues around trade justice people are not quite sure where they address themselves. There is a wide target area, so to speak.

My question about how NGOs relate to our existing international institutions has something to do with that. I am not saying we have no means of addressing the targets of international trade justice campaigns, but I don't think it is just a matter of bringing pressure to bear on electorates. There is another layer which has to do with what Professor Bobbitt was talking about earlier, in terms of the shift of balance from a system where regular democratic elections are the main focus, to a kind of continuing to and fro between institutions and populations across national boundaries and within international institutions.

Sir Mark Tully: This brings the discussion on to something which I think is of crucial importance – the manifest failure of the international governance system to deliver more equitable distribution of resources. How could the market state improve this?

Professor Bobbitt: The amount of money given in foreign aid by all states is a tiny fraction of the amount of money in the international economy. If we were able to reduce the interest rate on debt held in the Third World and developing states by even one per cent, it would be vastly larger than all the foreign aid given by every state to any state. Unless we can mobilise the market on behalf of developing states, then we will always be in the hortatory position of urging reluctant national publics that don't see their interest being served by what end up being pretty paltry amounts of assistance.

Market states can come in many varieties, and in the future, I am sure, will play out many variations. But I can imagine this: that the gap between rich and poor, though it may increase, will take place in a context of greater wealth generally so that the development gap actually closes. By that I mean, for example, that the people of the wealthier states will improve their longevity far less than those of the poorer states.

A redistributive regulatory agenda has one serious flaw for those it seeks to benefit. It tries to reorient the market, making the rich a little bit poorer to achieve a shrinking gap between rich and poor, when what we want to do is shrink the development gap and make the poor better off generally. Now, of course, in this country and in mine we are already quite wealthy. I went to a house-party in England many years ago where there was a fortune-teller who read my palm and said, 'You are going to be rich!' I thought, 'Gee, this is great!' I kept waiting, the years rolled by, but I was still a Law Professor and I thought, 'When is this payoff going to happen?' Well, suddenly it dawned on me that, like everyone in this room, I was already quite rich and that the really important step lay not in taking my riches and distributing to others, but in trying to see that my riches were used as best they could be to increase the ability of the market generally to raise the level of the desperately poor everywhere, and not just in my own society.

Lord Owen: I would like to challenge this 'market state'. What does it mean? I am in favour of markets, I have always championed them, but I have always done so in the context of a social market. I think there are things in a market state which can't be settled by markets, and the market state's record is pretty bad on redistribution. And is there something within the market itself which militates against redistributing, if you give everything over to competition?

The only way to discuss the market is to delineate that which is able to be dealt with in an open market, where there really is a genuine choice, and those areas where the market has to have some degree of management or where there is no place for the market at all. Just look at the situation in the agricultural market in the world. The two richest groupings, the United States and the European Union, both have deeply protectionist agricultural policies. We can argue about whether we in the European Union are worse than the United States – I personally think we are, slightly – but both are very bad indeed and show no signs of making any real significant change. Our political parties are too interested in pacifying the farmers' lobby, and we, for some reason, seem to be incapable of dropping these commitments. This is not a market, it is a commitment to a subsidy within the nation state that distorts global markets. In the case of the European Union, we are replicating it across 25 nation states. This is an example of where coming together in a regional framework has actually made protectionism a good deal worse.

Professor Bobbitt: Lord Owen draws his focus on something that I would like to address myself, and that is the difference between a market and a market state. A market state makes laws – markets don't do that. It is hardly a defence of the pre-existing system to say that protectionism is one of its products and is the classic manoeuvre of nation states whose interests are never global but always confined to a particular ethnic and cultural-linguistic group.

If the market state isn't a market, what is it? A market state uses markets but it does not cease being a state. As we have seen, states have moved from using conscription to all-volunteer armed forces; they have deregulated not only industry but women's reproduction; they have gone from welfare supplements to job training and labour programmes, or to top-up fees in this country. All are examples of states using the market.

I am not an ambassador for the market state. I come from the American South, where we have a backward-looking attitude towards change. We also have a story you probably haven't heard. It is from my part of Texas and is about a very beautiful, very ancient oak tree, with two mayflies on a leaf. One says to the other, 'I understand these leaves grow. At some point in the year, this tree is just budding with young leaves, and now it's covered with these large velvety things we are on.' And the other mayfly says, 'That's ridiculous! I have been on this leaf all my life and nothing has changed.'

Archbishop: If I may comment on this last exchange. The important point is that, if I hear the definition correctly, the market state is a way of talking about the *method* of delivering social cohesion or well-being, rather than reducing society to a market. It is not a value judgement saying markets are abstractly better than welfarist nation states of a certain generation, nor that this is the only model in society, but that the primary way in which people come to have confidence in their political institutions is increasingly dominated by a market model in which the citizen becomes very close to a consumer in relation to political power.

I don't think that Professor Bobbitt or others who have talked about this are saying this is necessarily a good thing to be sought – it is just something that is perceptibly evolving. If it is, the question is not how do we stop it or how do we turn the clock back, but who are the partners for the market state going to be in guaranteeing that it works justly, or comprehensively? That is a good question if the analysis is right that we are inexorably going towards a more consumerist approach to politics. How does the market state create the kinds of co-operation, conversation, collaboration, delivery and openness to critique that will prevent it from degenerating into a purely consumerist society?

Sir Mark Tully: If we are moving in this direction, don't we have to change the attitude of the consumers?

Archbishop: In the long run I would say yes. Meanwhile, assuming that the society in which everybody is instinctively committed to the welfare of their neighbour without hesitation is some way off, I think we have to look at how those groups, including religious groups, which are committed to a different kind of moral vision of human community, work both in solidarity and critically with such systems.

Sir Mark Tully: Now we come to questions from the audience. The first question is, 'What can be done practically to forestall groups that, for economic or political reasons, are excluded from politics and media access, from turning to nihilistic violence?' Perhaps that follows on from your remarks, Archbishop.

Archbishop: The question of exclusion is one of the most pressing that we face at the moment. I remember a point some years ago when people were talking in rather optimistic terms about the growth of community politics as national politics ceased to engage people. I thought at the time that this was a slightly dangerous polarity to get stuck with, and what we really needed to talk about was how larger-scale institutions and smaller-scale political action connected. If you don't have connection or communication between civil society groups, ethnic groups, local groups and the larger-level politics, both wither. One of the most destructive results is that sense of profound political alienation, which I think the questioner is addressing.

The same applies on the world stage. The fact that there can be no self-contained local politics on the world stage is an important consideration. Again, we face the issue of exclusion from the decision-making process.

Professor Bobbitt: I would like to see a world that was completely wired, a world in which every person could cheaply and easily get on the Internet and contact any other person. I think this would eventually transform the media. The media right now is very much like the nation state within which it grew, but it too will change. It has already adopted something of the role as a kind of institutionalised opposition to government, whether the government is from the right or left. I think it will undergo further change and be radically decentralised. So the way to get media access isn't to force Fox News to have revolving protesters appear every afternoon, but it's to empower the people who would like to contact other people electronically.

Sir Mark Tully: That's interesting because it takes us on to our second question, which is, 'What impact does the Internet have on Professor Bobbitt's market state groupings and on Lord Owen's nation states?'

Lord Owen: The Internet, in my view, is a perfect example of the market at work. The founders of it decided not to apply for patents, they did not constrict it and they did not create their own little commercial Internet, which they might well have done. That would have been the normal pattern. Instead, it became an open market, with absolutely open access.

I think the Internet is one of the great liberators and will change our world. It will bring people together. The fact of being able to speak and communicate across national boundaries is an important opener, particularly as the postal service gets worse. It's also a great educator. Doctors now are confronted by people in their surgeries who come in already having been extremely well briefed on the Internet. In the old days, a doctor could pat a patient on the head and give them a prescription. Now the person says, 'But what do this drug's side-effects do in relation to the other options I have?'

Through the Internet the UN has tried to make its debates more accessible. More accessible political dialogue is only to be encouraged. This is what I would call active democracy. But we have to face it, too, that in any democracy there are an awful lot of people who do not want to be involved, and that is their right.

Archbishop: I would like to put two questioning footnotes to the positive approach to the Internet here. I agree with what has been said. I think it is already changing our political culture in all kinds of ways for good and ill. But the Internet is not just something which comes out of mid air. The wiring up of the world has economic conditions; it doesn't happen unless you have certain kinds of economic provision. We also have to face the fact that the dependence of a political culture on something like this faces quite severe challenges should we be facing a major energy crisis, so this interlocks with issues which further debates in this series will take up.

Sir Mark Tully: There is a question which I think will particularly interest Lord Owen. This is about the United Nations Security Council's permanent membership: 'Should it be changed if it is to be relevant in the future?' As the questioner says, 'The five principal arms traders are also the permanent members.'

Lord Owen: That's true, by and large. The bigger countries tend to justify their arms expenditure by being able to sell abroad and cut their costs. There are exceptions. Even now South Africa is quite a large arms supplier. And, of course, because of the strange laws, Switzerland has for a long time been channelling arms through arms dealers. But I am not sure that that's the nub of the question really.

Sir Mark Tully: I think the nub is more about the United Nations.

Lord Owen: I think it would greatly improve world governance to have a much more representative Security Council than we have at the moment. I find it quite impossible to justify a world in which India, the largest democracy in the world, is not a member of the Security Council. And I don't believe that Pakistan can be allowed to effectively block India's position, or that of any of the other countries around it. I also think it is not realistic to expect Germany to go on being such a large contributor to the United Nations and all its agencies and not be recognised now, after all the time since the Second World War, as a country that deserves to be a permanent member of the Security Council. Similarly, for Japan. Then you have to look at other regions of the world and see if they can be permanently represented. Brazil is a very large country and the justification for it being a permanent member on a regional argument seems to be very strong indeed. Nigeria is the largest country in

Africa by a long way. It also has a very substantial Muslim population. Because everyone is in love with South Africa and Nelson Mandela, South Africa will be able to make a very strong case for representation, but I think it is logical that Nigeria should be a member.

We can all have fights about membership, but if the United States decided that enlargement of the Security Council was now one of the ways of improving global governance – and I think it would – it could be achieved. The Italians would object to the Germans coming in and various other countries would have various other lobbies – Indonesia will say, 'Why not us?' In terms of the big problem of better representation of Muslim countries, India has a very substantial Muslim population and so has Nigeria. I believe that enlargement to the five is very important.

Should they have veto powers? I don't think so. The veto arose as an accident of history and I believe it to be essential, even though it was very frustrating when used by the Soviet Union. But I think you have to accept the existing veto powers.

Professor Bobbitt: If I had agreed with Lord Owen before that the UN Security Council was, and would increasingly become, an able manager of the world security crisis, which I do not in fact agree with, my concept would have just evaporated after that last intervention. When you think of the difficulty we have had in getting the Council to act in all of the important and contesting regions in the last 15 years, to add to the Security Council Brazil, Nigeria, India, Japan, Germany, Indonesia …

Lord Owen: I didn't say Indonesia.

Professor Bobbitt: I would certainly include Indonesia, as you have to have someone from the East – it cannot make that task any easier. What is the source of the inability of the Security

Council? Rich, powerful states that have wide interests. Why do we have a veto system? Why does Lord Owen support it? Because he is speaking, as he should, for his nation. Britain has one and Britain will not give it up. France has one – completely unjustifiable – but France would never give it up. So the possibility of pouring more responsibility into a more complex Security Council is not one that fills me with the optimism that I am trying to summon up.

Archbishop: I am rather inclined to agree. I think that while enlargement has a great deal to be said for it, any enlargement of the Security Council or extension of the veto powers would be problematic. The defensibility of the existing veto system is equally problematic.

I want to look more broadly at the procedures and protocols of the Security Council and, as I hinted earlier, who has the right of access, who has the right to be heard, with whom must the Security Council consult outside itself? I would also like to ask questions about the implementation of Security Council resolutions. At the moment this is – well, if I say 'vague', that is putting it quite kindly. How the delivery is realised needs intense attention. It is not just about membership.

Sir Mark Tully: We come to a question which is very much for the Archbishop to start off with and is a very important one because so many people ask it: 'Are the world's religions the cause or the solution of global conflict?'

Archbishop: Probably both, but that is a very Anglican answer. Religion is, among many other things, a peg on which conflicts can be hung. Quite often it is something which intensifies conflicts whose roots are elsewhere. But because ethnic, community, national and international tensions are very seldom, if ever, caused by one set of factors, I think it's really just one of those empty slogans to say, 'Religions are responsible for dot,

dot, dot' – as well as assuming you know what you mean by 'religions'.

What people usually mean is that many wars in the history of Europe have been fought on religious pretexts, and one of the major ways in which some people construct major conflicts in the world now is between Islamic nations and the rest. Now, I don't accept either of those premises as they stand, but I'd say just two things. First, if it is true that religion is so easily factored into conflicts, it is imperative for anyone concerned with reconciliation and sustainable peace in the world to understand how religious communities work, and frequently people don't bother about this. We have caught up belatedly in the last few years in our public discourse in this country with the fact that religious motivation is not just a matter of private opinions held by a few eccentrics.

Second, and more positively, the work that is done by religious communities at the global level in trying to identify common values and common goals has been dramatic in recent years. The fact that I am able to go this coming weekend to Cairo to take part in some ongoing Muslim–Christian dialogue is the result of several years of work by lots of people who have worked harder than I to make possible these high-level exchanges. They have been patient and careful in outlining a vision for peace-making and repudiating revenge and violence, which can be pressed in the political sphere. I don't think it is an empty aspiration that religious communities worldwide should be able to play in the future a greater part in defining and pressing for these positive values. So I don't think the terms of 'Are religions good for you or bad for you?' as it's usually put, help us very much. We need deeper understanding. We need confidence in the ability of communities to reshape their vision in those ways.

Lord Owen: I am not sure I know how to answer that question. I think that for politicians, politics can sometimes degenerate into extremism, and fundamentalism and extremism are pretty closely linked. Unfortunately, religions often have very much the same zealotry attached to them and have done a great deal of harm.

We face a considerable problem at the moment about Islamic fundamentalism. I don't think that we can overcome this problem without changing some of our structures. It's been unfortunate but the world has accepted, it seems, that democracy in Arab countries and in many Muslim countries somehow does not seem to be possible. But India is a classic example of where that has not been the case for a Muslim country. Turkey is the other example.

Sometimes people ask, 'Well, what can we do?' To this audience I would say that we should take Turkey into the European Union. In doing so we are going to face difficulties, probably in our own pockets, but I cannot think of a single issue which would be more important in demonstrating to the Muslim world that we are serious about working across religious boundaries. It is an issue on which we may well have to mobilise our political parties, because there is beginning to be a fracturing of the consensus that was building up inside the European Union on this question. It is a tricky one, but I think rejecting Turkish membership could have very damaging consequences. This is an issue for us – members of the European Union – and we ought to be trying to take this next decision to open serious negotiations with Turkey, and we would be doing quite a lot to overcome some of those religious problems by doing so.

Sir Mark Tully: Now we come to our last question. The questioner talks about the United States not as a nation but an empire, and if it is an empire, 'What are the implications for balancing power economically, politically and militarily?'

Professor Bobbitt: I don't think the United States is an empire.

Calling it this reflects the fact that we are in a period of dramatic change and we are simply struggling to find new terms that really do apply.

I am a Law Professor and the idea of an empire has a very strong legal meaning. It means that the political leaders of the metropole at the centre control the civil life of the imperial subjects – where they go to school, what they study, what languages they learn, what religions they can practise. Now the imperial centre may decide it doesn't wish to make these choices, it may allow some greater or lesser freedom; but that's what it means to be an empire. Like all law, it is finally enforced by violence.

The United States' influence in Europe and Asia, however, is based on consent. For example, it is well known that the US has military bases all over the world – maybe as many as 170. These bases don't exist because we would fight the people whose countries house them. Indeed, as we are seeing in Germany, the threat to remove them has caused a great deal of consternation. When the US has had a base – and I have in mind the huge installation in Subic Bay – and a state like the Philippines asked for it to be removed, that is exactly what they did. Colin Powell put it very movingly when he said, 'The only territory the United States has ever asked for was the territory large enough to bury our dead.'

The fact that we have global interests and that tonight young men and women from my country and yours are making quite personal sacrifices, whether you agree with the policy or not, does not necessarily reflect the institutions that we had a century ago. There are other, newer models to grope for. I know that the US is often accused of being an empire, and sometimes we may act as though we have the swagger of the imperial about us. But if you look at the twenty-first century, those states that will exercise influence can only do so by consent. There is no future for an empire, American or otherwise.

Sir Mark Tully: Archbishop, do you believe America is an empire?

Archbishop: Not in the strict sense, but I am less sanguine here than Professor Bobbitt. I seem to be cast in the role of being gloomier than either of my colleagues tonight. Consent in relation to military installations, for example, seems to me only a small part of the difficulty we face. I agree, not 'empire'. But there are different forms of economic and cultural dominance which are not exhausted by either language of empire in the legal sense, or the consent of local governments to American representation. What is felt to be so difficult in many parts of the world is not the presence necessarily of American arms, but the presence of American culture. This is one of the major issues in the Islamic world. It is not simply about military installations, it is about cultural power.

There is also the sense, widely shared in the world, that it is the United States' economic priorities which determine aspects of its foreign engagement, and that this distorts, or warps, local economic life. Whatever the justification or otherwise of those perceptions, they are there, and that is why the language of empire is sometimes used in a kind of mythological way.

Sir Mark Tully: We are running out of time and I have to ask each speaker to make a last statement as a summing-up. Professor Bobbitt.

Professor Bobbitt: It is interesting that the discussion has come around at the end to the role of the United States, and whether or not the new form of state – the market state – has yet come, or if it hasn't, when will it and what will it be like? The future of both are quite intertwined.

The United States is the only state with truly global interests – military, economic, and political. The European Union is the only example of a functioning 'umbrella' of states that ought to allow for more decentralisation and for smaller communities. If the US and the European Union can, through the compromise and consensus that Lord Owen spoke of, and through deep reflection on our behaviour within our own societies, find examples for the future, we have it in our power to make the forms of the state that are evolving humane.

It may be an alliance of democracies. It may be a kind of G2 between the US and the European Union. But of this I am certain: if we do not act in the spirit of consensus and co-operation, world security – not just its physical and economic security, but its ability to choose a world of its own volition – will become far less achievable than it otherwise would be.

Lord Owen: There is a difference between compromise and consensus. Consensus is admirable and is often difficult to achieve. If we look at the situation over Iraq, there was no hope of reaching consensus in the Security Council, but we were much closer than many people realised to a compromise. The French were ready at one stage to compromise to the extent that they would not veto the British, Americans and others going into Iraq. They did not want the second resolution and they came to Washington and argued against it. It was actually the British that demanded, in a sort of rather selfish act, this second resolution because it would have given them the consensus which would have made it much easier politically.

We have to understand the necessity for compromise. In the European Union there is going to be a very urgent need to understand the necessity for more compromises with the United States, and there must be some response back. We are losing that capacity to understand the compromises that we have developed amongst ourselves. I do not believe America is an imperial power. Actually I spent most of my time worrying about America being isolationist.

Archbishop: I don't think that we shall see any viable world governance without channels and institutions being in place that allow a reasonable voice to all. That is not simply a voice for each nation but a voice for those groups that I have been speaking about this evening in terms of civil society and in terms, you won't be surprised to hear, of religious faith. The worst futures we could face would, I think, be those which are dominated by unchallengeable voices wherever they are to be found. The most viable transnational institutions are those which allow proper, mutually responsible, critical exchange between the world's communities. We are still some way from finding this.

Sir Mark Tully: We have had an absolutely fascinating discussion and have been given a lot to think about. Thank you all very much indeed.

Chapter Two

Is There an Alternative to Global Capitalism?

The second St Paul's Institute dialogue was held at St Paul's Cathedral on 15 September 2004 between Dr Rowan Williams, Archbishop of Canterbury, Professor John Kay and Dr Muhammad Yunus. It was chaired by Baroness Shirley Williams, Leader of the Liberal Democrats in the House of Lords, and formerly Secretary of State for Education (1976–79) and Professor of Elective Politics at Harvard University.

Baroness Williams: Good evening, ladies and gentlemen. Welcome to this next of the Archbishop's dialogues on the question, 'Is There an Alternative to Global Capitalism?' I am not one of the speakers but I shall just make a couple of comments. First, whereas, clearly, there are alternatives to global capitalism, they don't seem to work terribly well; and the second is, has global capitalism worked very well, given the almost obscene differences in the level of income and wealth throughout our world? These are issues of great importance to people who think deeply and, of course, not least also to people of the various faiths. I would like, if I may, to introduce you to our two protagonists.

Dr Muhammad Yunus was Professor of Economics at Chittagong University in Bangladesh. He has always been an economist who believes that theory should lead to practice, and he is probably most famous throughout the whole world for founding the Grameen Bank in Bangladesh, which gives many, many hundreds of thousands of poor people the opportunity to start their own enterprises, their own smallholdings, their own little businesses, by making credit available to them at a far lower cost than they would encounter from the formal banking system. So brilliant was the concept of Dr Yunus that it has now extended from the Grameen Bank to one kind of Grameen enterprise after another, both public and private, and has gone far beyond even Bangladesh to many other countries in Asia and Africa who have followed the path that Dr Yunus laid out. It is a great honour for us all that Dr Yunus has joined us this evening.

The second protagonist in our debate is Professor John Kay, who has a very distinguished record as a professor of economics and of business in a number of universities. Specifically, he was the Chairman of the Board of the London Business School. He was the first Director of the Said Business School at Oxford and is a Visiting Professor at the London School of Economics. Professor Kay has written widely on the subject of the financial and economic system of the world and, in particular, has written a book which has been very widely read, called *The Truth about Markets*. So we are very honoured to have also the presence here of Professor John Kay.

May I begin by asking Dr Yunus to speak on the subject.

Dr Yunus: Thank you very much. I am delighted to be here. It is a great experience for me to be in the Cathedral talking about something I feel very strongly about – the alternative to global capitalism. To me it is not the alternative to global capitalism as such, rather the alternative to the present form of global capitalism. I feel that capitalism is, as it is practised, a half-done story. It is not fully dialogued and there is plenty of room to build it up to its logical completeness.

Businesses that we see today are businesses to make money. That is the only kind of business that the present form of capitalism brings about. I feel that there is a complete other set that is missed out – that is, business to do good for people. While the business to make money recognises people's desire to make money and self-gain, we do not recognise people's willingness to share life with others. That part is completely missed out from capitalism as it is practised, not from the concept of capitalism as such.

There are lots of social entrepreneurs in the world, and social entrepreneurship is as old as human beings themselves. Anybody who would like to help another person is a social entrepreneur. Social entrepreneurship came into being on the basis of charity, where some kind of cost recovery in the work of helping others was introduced. Through social entre-preneurship 100 per cent cost recovery is possible; but the objective of the business is to help people, not to make money by the initiators themselves.

If we can meet 100 per cent cost recovery, then social entre-preneurship moves into a completely different level. That is what we may call social business entrepreneurship. Once we can make social business entrepreneurship recognised, then capitalism can become a complete set of ideas and practice.

There are many social entrepreneurs today, but they are not recognised because the present structures and theories don't have any room for social business entrepreneurship. We need to expand social business entrepreneurship by creating appropriate institutions where they are recognised and so that businesses can do good to people.

For example, the majority of the world's population do not have access to the services of the financial institutions. So that is a half-done story because we interpret that businesses can operate only for personal gain, personal profit. But if we could expand our financial institutions to embrace social business entrepreneurship, we could include every single human being.

If you take our experience at the Grameen Bank as an example of social business entrepreneurship, it is a perfectly capitalist structure reflecting capitalist institutions. But the objective of the bank is not to make money for ourselves – its objective is to help poor people create their own jobs and move on with their lives through business. The Grameen Bank makes a profit, but at the same time it can reach out to millions of people. Today, the Grameen Bank has 3.7 million borrowers, 96 per cent of whom are women. Our borrowers gradually move up from a very low level of business. The bank lends out over half a billion dollars each year in loans, with the average size about $200, and has a recovery rate of nearly 100 per cent.

There are enormous varieties of things that can be done through social business entrepreneurship. So if we can create the right institutions, capitalism will come to its logical conclusion. All the worries that we have now, by leaving capitalism in the hands of the profit-seeking, personal gain-seeking entrepreneurs, will be over because people will have the opportunity to benefit through the other type of capitalism.

It will need a different kind of stock market. The stock market that we have next to us here at St Paul's in the London Stock Exchange is a stock market for the people who are investing money to make personal gains. But perhaps there will be another stock market on the other side of the Cathedral which will be the stock market where people will come to invest money to do good to other people. And there will be a special type of rating agency to find out which organisations, which entrepreneurs, were doing good to people in terms of doing social good. So, in brief, what I am saying is that global capitalism can be remade to include the urge of human beings to help other people within the framework of capitalism itself. Thank you.

Baroness Williams: Thank you very much indeed, Dr Yunus. Professor Kay.

Professor Kay: It is a very great pleasure for me to be here, though I feel a little odd and difficult being in the centre of St Paul's as a defender of global capitalism. But actually, St Paul's is at the centre of one of the great financial centres of the world and, while there are buildings around us – the London Stock Exchange is just moving in opposite – where I might get an - easier reception for what I have to say this evening, I nevertheless think it at least as important to say it to this audience and in this place. I hope that I will be able to persuade you that there isn't as acute a dichotomy between the values of the market and your concerns as you may have thought when you walked in this evening.

Half of the population of the world lives on less than $1000 a year. And yet, if we think about that statistic for a moment, we know it can't quite be right, because if any of us in this Cathedral tonight were asked to live on £10 a week, we know we would not survive. We could not do it. So how does half the population of the world, who mostly do survive on these incomes, actually do it? They do it because they are very largely self-sufficient. They are not much engaged in the market economy. They produce most of their own food. They gather most of their own fuel. They are largely responsible for building their own housing. The women among them also gather food and cook it. They are very often responsible for the clothing of their families as well, and such education as people in these situations receive – and it is often not very much – is mostly provided by mothers.

People in this position don't do much else beyond produce food, fuel, housing – these basic necessities of life – for their own consumption. They don't do much else because they can't do much else. When you have spent your day doing these things, spent your day providing for yourself, you don't have time or energy left to do other things. Most of the poor people of the world are self-sufficient or they are part of very small self-sufficient groups.

Our lives are radically different from that, and the reason our lives are radically different is that we benefit from the kind of specialisation that Adam Smith, who first understood the mechanics of the modern market economy, called the division of labour. Smith went into a pin factory and described the extraordinary process by which, instead of one person making a pin from start to finish, it was broken down into a whole variety of processes in which people specialised and were, as a result, much more productive.

What we all do in our daily working and social lives is work in teams. By working in teams we produce far more than we could produce individually. By working in teams we develop, utilise and hone our own special talents. The world we live in today is one of incredible specialisms, in which it is not just that there are several people engaged in different operations in the pin factory. There is a man who buys insurance for the pin factory, and there is someone who answers the telephone in the pin factory. We live in a world in which people care for children so that the teachers, who are the mothers of these children, can go out and educate the children of yet other people. We live in a world which is the modern market economy, and which is characterised by specialisation and exchange.

If we understand that that is the basis of the modern economy, we realise two important propositions. Firstly, that we in the rich world are not rich because poor people in the poor world are poor, nor vice versa – they are not poor because we are rich. Secondly, poor people in the world today are not in the main poor because they are victims of the global economy. In fact it is the opposite: they are poor because they are not, as we are, part of that global economy.

Beside that somewhat bleak picture of half of the world living on $20 a week or less, there is actually quite a lot of good news. A few months ago I went to Iceland, which in the nine-teenth century was one of the poorest countries in the world. It is easy to see why because if you are self-sufficient, if you are gathering food and fuel for yourself, doing so in Iceland – even if you do it all the time – is something that gives only a very low standard of living. But today Iceland, Norway, Finland, these other Nordic countries, are no longer among the poorest in the world, they are among the richest. The reason they are among the richest is because of the specialisation I have described within the context of the global economy. These countries export fish, oil, paper and mobile phones. By selling these to other countries they are able to achieve some of the highest standards of living achieved anywhere. By being part of a global trading system they have become rich and prosperous.

Fifty years ago, South Korea was one of the poorest countries in the world. Today it is on the verge of joining the club of rich countries. The best news of all is that in the last decade more people have moved out of extreme poverty than in many pre-vious decades. They have done so as a result of the economic growth which has been happening in China and India, as these countries have been more drawn into the market economy and the global economic system. So the question we are asked tonight is, 'Is There an Alternative to Global Capitalism?' If that means, 'Is there an alternative to the market economy that creates rich and prosperous societies?' my answer is, 'No, there is not.'

The market economy characterised by what I have described (specialisation and exchange) is the only system which has been devised – and I think the only system likely to be devised – which is sufficiently productive to give large numbers of people a worthwhile life, and to relieve them from the burden of self-sufficient subsistence enough in order to do all the other things that make life worthwhile. In that sense there is no alternative to global capitalism.

There is no alternative to the market economy, but the

market economy which I have described exists, survives and develops because, and only because, it is embedded in a supportive political, economic and cultural environment. If we think of the market economy outside that environment, we learn why it does not work. We live in an *embedded* market economy, and that is the reason why we are rich. It is the only mechanism known to us today which is capable of making our societies rich.

Baroness Williams: Thank you very much, Professor Kay. Archbishop, it's your turn to comment on what you've heard.

Archbishop: Thank you very much. The question which, perhaps for many people, underlies the discussion tonight is not simply 'Is there an alternative?' but 'Does global capitalism as at present constituted work in the way it professes to work?' If there is no alternative to the global market, what are the choices we have about making it fulfil the goals which it professes to have – goals which are to do with access and inclusion and democratisation and all those other things?

I have one or two general questions to throw into the discussion and perhaps particular questions that my colleagues here might like to follow in further discussion. One of the things which currently makes global capitalism look or feel morally unacceptable to a lot of people has to do, I suspect, with the problems of unrestricted capital flow and short-term capital investment. Capital moving in and out of a national economy can change it radically and then leave people stranded. There are such stories and they need to be reflected on.

This is related to the second general issue which I guess people have moral questions about, and that is a point made by Joseph Stiglitz in some of what he has written on the subject. If the opening up of markets in economically developing countries focuses solely on liberalisation of the market, you may very well produce not an upward but a downward spiral of prosperity because of the lack of 'embeddedness', to pick up Professor Kay's very important word.

A third general reflection has to do with a world in which the unregulated drift of capital ends up creating what are often called security enclaves – a deeply disturbed, dysfunctional set of societies with no stake in the global economy because they haven't got onto the upward spiral, necessitating intensive and sometimes violent security in the states that have developed.

Now all of these are parts of the picture which some see developing or intensifying, and they are some of those areas that cast a moral shadow over the picture that is often put of the benign effects of a global market. So, to my specific questions, I would like to hear more from Professor Kay about how developing economies, currently disadvantaged, become agents in the global economy without that paralysing moment where short-term investment, liberalisation without context, actually drives people further down. How do we overcome that? Then to Dr Yunus, the significance of enterprises like the Grameen Bank is enormous, and my own view of the opportunities and potential of different sorts of micro-credit is very sanguine. But how does it become possible for micro-credit institutions to receive adequate resourcing and backing both from classical banking institutions and from governments in a way which doesn't leave them, in turn, stranded, adversely affected by larger-scale movements? If I can pick up the same word again, what is the appropriate *embeddedness* of the micro-credit institutions in the wider global context?

Baroness Williams: These are very challenging questions, and I will start with Professor Kay.

Professor Kay: Let me emphasise again that word 'embeddedness', because what I am attempting to argue is that the market economy functions because, and only because, it does so in the context of a whole set of supportive community, social and political institutions. The micro-credit movement is in itself one example of that. It works precisely because it is embedded in the society in which it operates.

But we can see in the contrast between the evolution of the two great communist regimes, after communism in them collapsed, the difference between two ways of operating. Perhaps for me the biggest puzzle of world economic history is that 200 years ago rapid economic development began in Western Europe and not in South-East China, because in so many objective ways the conditions in these two areas of the world at the time were the same. In a sense, the problem of China is not to explain why it is growing so quickly now but why it has been so poor for so long. Indeed, the success of Chinese people outside the massively dysfunctional political structures that have characterised China for the last two centuries is in itself a demonstration of how many of these conditions were in place. So with the right kind of political, social and cultural environment, and by accepting some of the institutions of the market economy, economic growth can happen very rapidly and bring prosperity to large numbers of people quite quickly, as it is actually today doing in parts of China.

On the other hand, in Russia we see the adverse consequences of the attempt to import a very naïve and simplistic view of how market institutions work into a country which lacked many of those political and social preconditions for doing so. If we look across Europe we can see progress in the Czech Republic, in Poland and Hungary, countries which are, as it were, close to the heartland of Europe and which will be assimilated very quickly into the group of rich countries of Western Europe. In Russia it is proving a much longer process, and a process much less likely to be crowned by success because it is so much harder to embed these institutions effectively. Market institutions only work within the right kind of context, and the prosperity we enjoy is as a result of the co-evolution of a whole variety of economic institutions with a range of political and social institutions as well.

Baroness Williams: Thank you very much. Dr Yunus.

Dr Yunus: First let me make a few comments. Just one comment on Professor Kay's remark about the reasons for poverty. If you talk to the poor people in a country you hear about the traditional crafts and work they do. There are basket-makers, farmers, day labourers, rickshaw-pullers, boatmen, and so on. They are the most specialised workers you can think of, and generation after generation do exactly the same thing. If you want to look at the division of labour, all you need to do is visit one village in Bangladesh or India and you will see the whole village divided by specialisation – the part where the weavers live, the part where the well-pressers live, the part where artisans and those with other kinds of trades live. They are very specialised; so lack of specialisation is not the cause of poverty.

The cause of poverty is on the institutional side, not at the personal level. Persons are the victims of the institutions. Persons don't cause poverty. Poverty is not caused by poor people themselves; it is something coming from outside, from the institutional rejection of poor people. Take the case of farmers in poor countries. They are specialised, but the rich countries close their doors to them: 'No, you can't sell your agricultural product to our country – we want to keep our agriculture to ourselves,' they say. So wealthy countries promote specialisation but shut the door when some poor countries want, through their specialisation, to sell their product to wealthy countries. So specialisation breaks down right there.

I would also like to say something about resourcing. Currently we are never in an embarrassing situation where we are getting more money in our branches than we can use to provide micro-credit to the poor. We don't want to send out an excess of money to the Central Office of the Grameen Bank in

Dhaka to invest in Dhaka, because I am always opposed to taking money from the rural areas and passing it on to be used by richer people in the metropolitan areas, where there is no shortage of money. We explain to people in rural areas that if they put their money in the Grameen Bank it will be used to lend to the poor people in that area so that the local economy will be built up.

So why doesn't micro-credit flourish if it is so easy – if you don't even have to bring money from Dhaka to a remote village but use local money that is already available? The reason is the legal framework. The problem of poverty is on the institutional side. The law doesn't allow you to take deposits. The law doesn't allow Micro-Finance Institutions (MFIs) to take deposits. The moment deposits are allowed, then you don't need money to be coming from outside. It is a resource which is available right there. So we go to the government and say, 'Why don't you create a law?' We go to the legislators and tell them, 'Why do you have to call them MFIs? Why don't you call them Micro-Credit Banks, because they have already shown how beautifully they do it? Conventional banks cannot come anywhere near it.'

In Bangladesh there is a very strange situation. All the conventional banks lend money to the very rich people in Bangladesh and they don't pay back! It is amazing. All the top people in the country are loan defaulters. One of our finance ministers decided to publish the list of the defaulters, and when you read it, it is almost the *Who's Who?* of the country! Some people get a little upset because their name doesn't appear on the list! So this is the kind of banking we are talking about, although the argument for not lending to poor people is that they will not pay you back.

Look at all the micro-credit programmes around the world – they have very nearly 100 per cent repayments. But nobody looks at this. Nobody would allow you to do banking – you cannot come anywhere near it. So resources are not the constraint. The legal framework is the constraint.

So why don't we change the law? We have been saying this over and over again. Hopefully it will come in Bangladesh and other countries. But conventional banking law is not going to be useful for micro-credit banking, as they are completely different. One is dependent on collateral, the other is dependent on legal instruments so that you can take the person to the court. Micro-credit doesn't involve taking anybody to court; it is based entirely on mutual trust. You cannot design a mutual trust-based banking system by bringing the law from the other type of banking; you must start with a completely new mindset.

Another issue is the international aid programme. The Department for International Development (DFID) gives money to the poor countries to help the poor people. The world as a whole gives over $50 billion a year to help poor people. How much of this goes into micro-credit? The World Bank's financing of micro-credit is less than one per cent of its $20-plus billion annual aid portfolio.

So this is the issue: how we make micro-credit happen. Micro-credit not only lends money, it affects the lives of people. The housing conditions of poor people are changed for the better by micro-credit. In the Grameen Bank, 100 per cent of the children of our customers are in school, because this is part of the programme that we've built up. It is built into our culture that if you receive micro-credit from the Grameen Bank, you send your children to school. The bank gives over 6000 scholarships every year to the brightest students. Today, families who never before could send their children to school have children in colleges, universities, medical schools and engineering schools. The bank gives educational loans to those students so that a completely new generation of educated children is coming up in those families. That is why I am insisting on social business entrepreneurship. You can run any business, not just micro-credit, in this way. Micro-credit is one example. Information Technology is another resource. If poor people can have access to information, they will change their whole life. They are very creative, very energetic people who work the hardest, but opportunities are not there for them.

Baroness Williams: There is just time on the top table here for another brief round, so I will start with the Archbishop, who may have further questions to put to Professor Kay and Dr Yunus.

Archbishop: Thank you for the responses to my original questions. I want to connect the two responses, because what Dr Yunus has been saying about trust is really a way of saying that where and how micro-credit works has a great deal to do with the vigour and resourcefulness of local civil society which can own the process, and that relates yet again to this crucial question of embeddedness.

Micro-credit cannot be imposed, created out of nothing. It presupposes a context of trust which can be reinforced, but not just made, by a legal environment. But I am still left with some questions about what it is that a vulnerable society can do in our world at the moment to protect itself against the dangers of contextless, non-embedded liberalisation. What was it possible for Russia to do to guard against the evil consequences of an unfettered market importation? What is it possible for a small or medium-sized African state to do in these circumstances, given that the actual powers of any government in the global economy now, as we were saying last week, are very limited? What is available to ward off the real dangers here?

Professor Kay: The Archbishop has identified a key element in this discussion, which is the extent to which the function of economies depends on trust. If we forget that, and if we follow – as people have been inclined to do in the last decade – the model of Western capitalism that says it is about encouraging people to be extremely greedy and imposing as few restrictions as possible on what they do, then that undermines that basis of trust. We have seen the very visible consequences of that in corporate collapses and scandals.

We have the same problem in Bangladesh, where Dr Yunus described the pattern of specialisation that exists within the villages of that densely populated society, but does not exist sufficiently generally across Bangladesh for it to be possible for economic institutions to develop that are effective in embracing the economy as a whole. Instead, the economy is operating at the level of these still largely self-sufficient, individual villages.

The development of trust is one of the key elements in this embeddedness of the market economy. What we have done so successfully in Western Europe has been to create both economic institutions and political institutions in which it is possible to have not complete trust, but quite a high degree of trust.

So what should we have done in Russia? It is easier to start saying what we should not have done in Russia, which is to create at the first possible opportunity highly liberalised, highly liquid capital markets and transfer all properties as rapidly as you can to private ownership. We have seen the consequence of the view that it doesn't matter much who owns the assets so long as some private individuals do, and these consequences in Russia have not been benign. So I am not going to offer any naïve remedies for how one can create these structures in Russia or in Africa. Indeed, I think the central starting point in thinking about how the market economy works is to say that there isn't going to be a blueprint for how to develop a successful market economy. It is precisely because a successful market economy is embedded, that the only way you can create it is by having simultaneous developments of political and social institutions with economic ones. That is why the business of creating it – whether in Africa or in Russia – is a much slower and longer process than any of us would like it to be. But what we need to learn is that if people come along telling us they have quick fixes to these problems, whether an extreme liberalisation or by virtue of development programmes sponsored from the West, any quick fix is certainly wrong – it misunderstands the nature of the problems and the institutions we are trying to deal with.

Baroness Williams: Thank you very much. Dr Yunus.

Dr Yunus: One principle I always believe in, when you say something is 'open', is that it sounds like everybody has the right to use it. In reality it is open only for the biggest or the richest. The poor don't have access. When you have globalisation it is exactly the same, meaning that now everybody's goods and services can move from anywhere to anywhere. But really the biggest and the most powerful have access and others don't. It is a super-highway of the world trade, but a highway for the big guys who can have their heavy trucks to go through those highways, not the Bangladeshi rickshaws that will be blown away – they don't have the right.

So you open up something without having any kind of traffic police. If you have a highway, as globalisation is a highway, then you need traffic control of the whole system – otherwise it's not globalisation, it is just opening up for colonisation of another kind.

The other part of capitalism has to be built, equally efficient and equally strong – that is the capitalism for doing good to people. It will run like a business, it will compete with business to make money, so it will be a fight among the equals, but it is run by people with social consciousness. They are doing it because they want to protect the poor, they want to do good to people, they want to help people take advantage of globalisation rather than get drowned by it. So this is what we need to do: have networks of good-intentioned people who build businesses instead of sitting in the sideline saying business is bad and walking away. If business is bad, we have to get in and make it good. We need lots of social business entrepreneurs.

Baroness Williams: We turn over to questions in a moment, but as the only politician on this panel, I can't forbear to avoid two sentences. One of the things that has emerged – and I think very importantly – is that an economic system, to work well, has to be embedded in a political and legal system that is fair and just and inspires trust. I am sure that Professor Kay would agree with me that one of the things always to remember about Adam Smith is that he lived in what was probably the most advanced civic society in the eighteenth century, namely Edinburgh, where people had a very strong sense of public service and brought that to bear on the development of the market.

The other point I want to make, again as a politician, is that it is very hard to divorce the concept of globalisation and the free market from structures of power. We might wish to do so, but it is unrealistic. If you look at the structures of power – the World Bank, the International Monetary Fund, the World Trade Organisation – as Dr Yunus has wisely said, it is quite clear that to a great extent the bargains that are made reflect the power of those who make them and not just the objective position of a free global market.

The first question from the audience that I have before me is, 'Do you think the West should help less developed countries to set up the political, economic and social environment necessary for a market economy to thrive?' I'll put that question first to Professor Kay.

Professor Kay: I think the simple answer to that is 'Yes.' But being a professor, you will expect me to qualify that answer, so I immediately will.

I think it really is important that we understand that institutions are the key to prosperity and, therefore, if we are to help other countries, that help is primarily in relation to building these institutions. But equally, we should understand that our capacity to build other countries' institutions from here is very limited and other countries will, quite rightly, resent our attempt to build these institutions in their environments.

So, yes, we should help them to do that, but we should understand the limitations both of our ability to do so and of their receptiveness to our attempts to do it. And most of all, we need to understand better what it is about our own institutions that actually works. A large part of the problem in this area, particularly in the last decade, has been that we have been in the grip of a very naïve over-simplified caricature of how our own market economy works. Selling that model to countries elsewhere in the world is both resented by them and not very successful when they attempt to adopt it. That's why, in the ten years after the West won the Cold War, the legitimacy of capitalism is, if anything, more under question today than it was before.

Archbishop: I warm very much to what has just been said and think the questions we have to ask are not so much, as you say, 'How do we create institutions over there?' but 'What is it in our practices and other practices where we have some say that frustrates the development of civil society institutions and civic trust elsewhere?'

There are two issues where we do have some say, and some choices. One, you won't be surprised to hear, has to do with the whole issue of debt. The impact of international debt on the development of civic society institutions, on education and on health care, is colossal. The burden of debt is one of the factors that drives, or has driven, some countries, not least in Africa, into the downward spin of militarisation. So we need to ask some very tough questions about the handling of debt relief.

Secondly, the apparently endemic protectionism of so much of the West in relation to developing economies simply frustrates not only economic development but the social and political development that is being spoken of. So, I say 'Yes' to co-operation in the developing world towards creating a more robust set of embedding institutions. But I also have some questions about our own political and economic choices in respect of what frustrates that development on the ground.

Baroness Williams: Thank you, Archbishop. Dr Yunus.

Dr Yunus: The key to developing economies is in the hands of the World Bank and the IMF. The West is trying to fix up every-thing in the Third World countries. The Asian Development Bank, African Development Bank and Inter-American Bank – they are there to fix up everything in the ways they think fit. And I would say they are doing it in the wrong way – by fiat, by orders. So we need to see how to make development happen with mutual consultation, with equal participation.

Baroness Williams: Thank you very much. The next question has been asked by a number of people: 'What does the panel think about the feasibility and desirability of implementing the Tobin Tax on currency speculation?' Professor Kay.

Professor Kay: I don't know whether everyone in the audience knows what the Tobin Tax idea is. The Tobin Tax is an idea formulated 30 or 40 years ago by James Tobin, a Nobel Prize-winning American economist, whose idea was essentially of having a very low-rate tax on all financial transactions – the kind of things that these guys over there in dealing rooms in the City do. His objective in formulating that tax was not to raise revenue – he didn't expect the tax would raise loads of revenue – but to slow down and reduce the quantity of financial market speculation.

My own view is that this is a highly desirable objective, and if a low-rate tax of the kind he described would actually work in bringing about that effect, I would support it. But I don't think there is actually the slightest practical chance of making a tax like that operate in today's complex, modern, financial markets, where transactions can take place electronically offshore and be done by the most complicated instruments anyone could imagine. Therefore, while I think the idea of putting some sand in the wheels of short-term international finance is a good one, that particular mechanism for doing it is one that doesn't fly.

Baroness Williams: Dr Yunus.

Dr Yunus: On the desirability, I am all for it. This is definitely one good way to raise lots of money. But I would like to know more: who handles this money, how this money is handled, for what purpose is it used, and so on.

With regard to its feasibility, I do not know the technicalities of how to make it effective, so I will stop there.

Baroness Williams: Thank you. Archbishop.

Archbishop: The problem has been identified very clearly of whether this would be in any sense an effective sanction in the present economic climate. The answer has to be, it doesn't look very likely. But if we are right in identifying unrestricted capital flow and excessively short-term capital investment as among the major engines of disadvantage, we are going to need another Nobel Prize-winning economist to help us out with a more effective form of sanction, because this continues to cripple and disadvantage states.

Baroness Williams: Thank you very much indeed. I should let on that I knew James Tobin very well and I think he did come up with a practical scheme, but that's an argument we will have on another occasion. The next question many people have asked, and is this: 'Is economic growth sustainable?' Professor Kay.

Professor Kay: The simple answer to that is 'Yes.' But I think what is in the minds of the people who are asking the question is the notion that we are going to come up against a variety of resource constraints which make it impractical to sustain economic growth at the pace which we have enjoyed in the Western world for the past two centuries. Our experience so far is that throughout these two centuries people have been saying that sort of thing and market economies have been endlessly inventive in finding ways of avoiding these resource shortages.

There is a classic book from 1866 on *The British Coal Trade* by the great economist of the time, Jevons, which explained why economic growth was bound to be brought to a halt by the world's insatiable demand for coal. He went on to say this might last until 1880 or 1890 – the coal might even carry on until 1910 or 1920 – but sooner or latter the coal was bound to run out. We can actually compare his projections of the world demand for coal in 1960 with what we know the world demand for coal actually was in 1960, and the answer is, he was out by a factor of ten. We should never underestimate the resourcefulness of market economies. Their resources are not unlimited, but are very far from being exhausted.

Dr Yunus: I will just take the other view. Growth is not sustainable until we become really conscious about how we deal with our environmental issues. We cannot just go on ignoring the environment, saying resources are unlimited, and that we can do anything we want. Who cares whether people from poor countries will one day ask the question, 'How come you used up all the resources of the world, while when we come into the picture, we have nothing left for us?'? So that question has to be resolved. It not only has to be sustainable today, it has to be sustainable for generations, it has to be sustainable across borders everywhere. All the social issues have to be addressed in order to make economic growth sustainable.

Archbishop: There are three things that make me less sanguine than Professor Kay. The first is the point just made by Dr Yunus, that there is an issue about the environment, about renewable resources. This is a kind of trailer for next week's discussion, but I see no way of realistically denying or ignoring the rapid spiral of environmental crisis in which we are now caught. If we take that seriously we, at the very least, have to talk about the rate of economic growth that we can expect.

Second, again hinted at by Dr Yunus, the expanding gap between rich and poor in at least one plausible scenario for the near future itself becomes an economic problem.

Third, one of the reasons for the collapse of the Soviet Union was that the demands of keeping up with the pressures around security and defence issues crippled economic possibilities. Imagine a world in which those security pressures spiralled again further, partly because of the growing economic gap. Economic growth cannot, I believe, continue in detachment from the possibilities of major crises around resourcing security. So with those three in mind, I am less hopeful – or perhaps more hopeful that we might be able to do things differently, but that's another story.

Baroness Williams: The next question is, 'Since there is a global movement towards localisation in response to the inhuman effects of the concentration of economic and political power, how is this consistent with global capitalism?' I will start with Dr Yunus and then Professor Kay.

Dr Yunus: Global capitalism is a blind force. It understands only the bottom line. It doesn't see what is good for you. So we must look at global capitalism in a more humane way, and make human concerns an equal partner and equal competitor so that the human element overcomes the rough and cruel edges of global capitalism.

Professor Kay: I would like both to agree and to disagree deeply with what Dr Yunus has just said. People have asked me, when I have made the kind of propositions I have been making tonight, 'But what about the profit motive – what Dr Yunus describes as the bottom line – isn't that what makes global capitalism work?' And the truth is, no, it isn't.

It isn't unrestrained greed that makes global capitalism work. Indeed, there are some countries in the world which are characterised by unregulated economic activity and unrestrained greed – countries like Nigeria and parts of modern Russia – and they don't work. Market economies function, as we have been saying so often, only within a context of trust and well-ordered political and social institutions. That is true of all the richest countries in the world, not only Norway and Switzerland, which are at the top of the income scale, but also the United States, where this model of cowboy capitalism actually bears no relation to the reality of how, beneath it, the American economy actually works.

So when Dr Yunus talks about an alternative model of how business operates around the world, I don't see that evolving, and I don't see how it could evolve as a network of different kinds of businesses in competition with the existing structure of bottom-line-orientated businesses. What I think we need to do is understand that successful business really operates by the inspiration of people, both chief executives and ordinary people working for companies, who really want to build great companies and to do good business. What motivates most people – while none of us are purely altruistic but, equally, few of us are purely selfish – is the desire to do a good job. The real model of capitalism we should be developing is therefore one which exploits that motive as much as possible and gives maximum scope to people to exercise that particular natural human desire.

Archbishop: The question points up one of the great paradoxes of our time: that the anti-globalisation movement depends in many ways on deploying the resources of a global market and a global communication system, with the economic assumptions that lie behind that. And I look back to discussions about the nature of politics in my days as a student and after, in the 1960s and early '70s, when there was a great interest at one point in the priority of community politics over the tired national political institutions – the parties. The trouble with that, of course, is that you can't pretend that large-scale institutions have no power or influence just by turning away from them. In some sense, lines of communication have to be kept open between the local and the large scale and global. And global institutions, as we have been reminded this evening, have in some ways to be made to work for local good and local concern.

I was glad to hear earlier mention of the World Bank and how it needs pressing towards resourcing the local, at the micro-credit level. And I suppose, if I can be permitted a theological aside, the balance of the local and the universal, the congregational and the global, is precisely one of those matters which all Christian churches are constantly wrestling with, whose distortions and imbalances are quite familiar. It would be quite interesting to have a discussion putting those experiences side by side, recognising that there is no vital and self-renewing local life without global resources, and that there is no just and legitimate global pattern without the deployment of local power and local creativity.

Professor Kay: The paradox of the global market economy is that nobody actually controls it. That is what is in some senses its strength, but it also makes people very angry – they throw stones at meetings of the World Bank or the World Trade Organisation in the belief that they have found the people who control the world economy. But the truth is that no one controls the world economy, or is ever likely to, and that's why there won't be Dr Yunus' traffic policemen either. The Internet is the most extraordinary creation of the last decade, but it is a model of worldwide communication on a massive scale that is controlled by nobody at all, and that is the way in which our economic systems function.

Baroness Williams: Professor Kay is leading with his chin, but I am not going to allow either of the other protagonists to take a poke at it, because I want to come to the two final questions. One I would ask my panel to be very brief about, is a practical question: 'What do you think of commercial banks getting involved in micro-credit/social entrepreneurship?' A quick answer, please. I will start with Dr Yunus.

Dr Yunus: Why not? We are inviting them all the time. I say, 'Why are you standing by? Come on, it is a good business. Come and join us. You are welcome!'

Professor Kay: I would agree with Dr Yunus and, in fact, this model of local community lending is something which, even in rich countries, is one of the mechanisms by which a lot of the credit obtained by poor people comes into being.

Archbishop: In poor communities it would be a great pity if there were a stark alternative between micro-credit and classical banking. If there could be co-operation and resourcing between the two, as one of my questions earlier was hinting, so much the better, I'd say.

Baroness Williams: I will conclude with what I might call a double-barrelled moral question: 'What would you say are the values needed in institutions for markets to work effectively and beneficially?' I will particularly look to Professor Kay on that one, coupled with this question, and I will particularly look at the Archbishop: 'Does the Gospel have anything to say about alternatives to global capitalism?'

Professor Kay: On the first question, we have already talked at some length about the value of trust. We also need to have a value of respect for people as individuals. One of the things that has been so destructive of many organisations in the last decade has been the attempt to rely on purely instrumental motivation, in the belief that people behave fundamentally individual-istically. Perhaps the most important value of all for me is that people who work in business should have as their objective the ideal of creating great businesses. If that sounds banal, it is quite different from a variety of conventional wisdoms.

When I say it's to create great businesses, what I mean is that above all it is to produce goods and services that people want. Secondly, it is to provide satisfying employment for people and returns to investors, and it is to operate in such a way that it benefits the community within which it operates. For me, a successful business is measured by success in all these dimen-sions, and that's much wider than the claim that the purpose of business is to maximise shareholder value of some kind. Business run on that basis can never command the kind of legitimacy that is needed to make either the business or capitalism as a whole successful.

But it is also narrower than saying that business is there in society to do good. Not only do I not think business has the obligation to do good, I don't think it has the right to do good. I am very frightened of the idea of the people who run large corporations regarding it as proper or legitimate for them to engage in their own particular conception of what it is a good society might be – that is a job for other people.

Dr Yunus: Well, we go in completely different ways on that sub-ject. As long as the bottom line of business remains only the maximisation of profit, then we are in trouble. That's why I say other types of businesses need to be created, where the bottom line is the maximisation of the social benefit. Unless we do that, as I described earlier, capitalism remains blind and will be very harmful.

Archbishop: On values, for markets to work effectively and constructively requires four things. Trust, obviously. Inclusion – that is, drawing an ever-increasing number of people in to have their place at the table. Patience – the systematic refusal of short-term solutions, short-term perspectives. And fourthly, a consistent refusal once again to think that economic man is a definition of any real being on the face of the globe.

There was a question about the Gospel. Two things I might put in there. The New Testament in general, never mind just the Gospels, seems to work with a model of human community in which the prime determinative vision is, 'All gifts are given so as to be given again.' The second thing which the Gospels in particular say pretty bluntly is: acquisitiveness kills – literally as well as spiritually.

Baroness Williams: Thank you very much indeed. It is nice for me as Chairman just to conclude with a few remarks. First of all, we are most grateful to the audience for coming. Thank you very much indeed. We had some marvellous questions and I am very sorry we had more than we could possibly handle, but thank you very much indeed for them. They were very perceptive and I think very much to the point. Secondly, it is my pleasant duty to thank what I think has been a remarkable panel of extremely thoughtful protagonists, and I hope you have enjoyed it as much as I have.

Chapter Three
Environment and Humanity: Friends or Foes?

The third St Paul's Institute dialogue was held at St Paul's Cathedral on 21 September 2004 between Dr Rowan Williams, Archbishop of Canterbury, Dr Mary Midgley and Dr Ricardo Navarro. It was chaired by Canon Lucy Winkett, Precentor of St Paul's Cathedral.

Canon Winkett: Good evening, and welcome to St Paul's Cathedral. Our two interlocutors for tonight's discussion with the Archbishop of Canterbury are Dr Mary Midgley and Dr Ricardo Navarro. Dr Mary Midgely is one of the UK's most distinguished moral philosophers and has been described as 'our foremost scourge of scientific pretension'. Formerly Senior Lecturer in Philosophy at Newcastle University, Dr Midgley has written extensively on the relationship between humanity and nature. Her numerous books include *Wickedness* and *The myths we live by*.

Dr Ricardo Navarro founded CESTA – which is now El Salvador's largest non-governmental organisation – in the

middle of the 13-year civil war, to promote grass-roots con-
servation strategies. His many achievements include preventing
toxic waste dumping by foreign powers in his country and
working with young people to plant a 'forest of reconciliation'
on war-damaged land. He was formerly Professor of
Engineering at the State University in San Salvador and, until
2004, Chair of Friends of the Earth International.

Could I ask you to give us your opening statements?

Dr Midgley: Dr Navarro will be telling you the appalling facts of
the state of our planet, so I shan't talk about those. I want to
explore the psychology that gives rise to our attitudes to the
planet. Why don't we believe that there is something wrong? If
we *really* believed it, we would be doing something about it, but
we are not. Why were people astonished in the spring when
the government's chief scientist, Dr David King, made the
obvious remark that climate change was a greater menace
than terrorism? Why, indeed, did the government try to silence
him?

Obviously, one reason for ignoring the facts is that it is
always inconvenient to change one's way of life, especially if one
is rather rich, as we all are now. I think, though, that there is
something deeper than that, which I want to dwell on tonight.
This is the unreal idea we have had about what the earth is.
There is a very old thought that the earth is the opposite of
heaven and that this life here is merely a passage to the next life,
which is the only important one. The earth, then, is seen as
something that stands in our way when we try to get to heaven.
This was the way the early Christians thought, because, along
with many others at the time, they believed that the world was
coming to an end shortly. In addition, the early Christians were
persecuted and martyred, so it made sense to look towards
something greater and better that was not of this world.

This way of thinking and talking persisted in our culture for
some time. It now seems old-fashioned, and you may think that

that idea cannot be what causes us now to neglect the earth. Surprisingly, however, at the Enlightenment, although many religious notions were abandoned, this one really wasn't. The idea took on a new form, but it amounted to the same thing as far as the earth was concerned. People stopped thinking of themselves as souls that would go up to heaven, and instead they thought of themselves as minds that lived in a higher sphere, independent of the earth, and so clever that they could control everything. This is still an extraordinarily prevalent way of thinking today.

One illustration of this separation between humanity and the earth is the fantasy of space migration. This is the notion that not only might a few spacecraft be sent up occasionally to some planet, but that we could, as a species, just go and live somewhere else if things became too inconvenient down here. You hear this suggested by a great many sophisticated people who ought to know better. When you stop and think about it, the notion is nonsense, but it is there and it shows just how independent we believe ourselves to be.

When Darwin published his ideas, what shocked people most was not that he seemed to be leaving out God, but that he was connecting us human beings so closely with the other animals of this planet. It was that earthly ancestry that was found to be so disconcerting. Disraeli asked the question: 'Is man an ape or an angel?' and he declared himself to be on the side of the angels. Now this sort of thing may sound like casual poetry, but I think that it shows a very deep habit of thought. We stand the best chance of changing our habits of thought and habits of feeling. We cannot directly change our ways of life unless we first start to imagine things differently and see them differently and feel differently about them.

I am very partial to the concept of Gaia, of the earth as a vast system of life which is self-maintaining and self-moving. Once we take that idea at all seriously, and see that we are a tiny part of it, we simply drop the thought of ourselves as independent separate beings. It is that unity with the rest of life that, it seems to me, we need.

The idea that we are independent, separate beings shows itself in so many ways in our lives today. I would like to end by appealing to you to look around for which bits of your life this idea still controls. It is really self-worship, a foolish conceit that prevails in human culture. We should watch for it in ourselves and draw attention to it when other people show it.

Dr Navarro: There are 25 million or so species on the planet. All of them take from nature only what they need to survive, except the human being. Humans are trained to take more and more from nature, the more power we have. What are the consequences of this?

Half of the forests that were once upon the face of the earth are gone, which means that many biological species are in danger of extinction. Many places are running out of water. The climate is changing. The use of petroleum is poisoning the air. In my country, for example, the air is so polluted that the leading cause of death is respiratory disease. The second commonest cause of death is gastro-intestinal disease from the water. The most dangerous thing you can do in my country, and in many Third World countries, is to breathe the air. The second most dangerous thing to do is to drink the water, and the third is to eat the food.

Humans are consuming so much petroleum that carbon emissions are creating climate change. In Central America in 1998 we had Hurricane Mitch, which killed 12,000 people in three days. The following year in Venezuela, 25,000 people were killed in three days. In 2000 in India a tornado killed 30,000 people in a couple of days. As you know, climate change makes these weather extremes stronger and more frequent.

We are running out of oil. In 40 more years we won't have petroleum, and knowing that motivates us to go to war. That is why we invaded Iraq, and I believe that going to Iraq to kill people was a criminal action. It cannot be justified. It is the consequence of our over-consumption of petroleum.

On the global level we are using twice as much water from underground aquifers than is being replenished. Sooner or later we will not have enough water. Currently one and a half billion people don't have clean water to drink – and I mean water to drink, not water to swim in. Half of humanity doesn't have sanitation facilities. Water is now becoming a cause of war. In the Middle East, for example, Israel does not want to leave some places, not because of the oil, but because of the water there. In Brazil and Paraguay we have the largest water aquifer in the world. President Bush said six months ago that the people from Al Qaeda are heading towards Latin America. We have to be careful – the Americans will want to militarise Brazil and Paraguay on that pretext. They will not find Al Qaeda there, they will find water. Bush went to Iraq, he didn't find weapons of mass destruction, he found oil. We know that already. The demand for water doubles every 20 years. Water will increasingly be a source of violence in the world, and in many local areas it is already that.

The demand for minerals is also a source of trouble. For every beautiful gold ring we buy, there are 12 tons of waste somewhere in the world generating problems – in South Africa maybe, or in Chile. Every time we buy diamonds we are contributing to wars in places such as Sierra Leone. We ought to remember that.

The impact of our consumption is not uniform. There are gross inequities. What kind of a social system is it that allows 25 per cent of the world's population to consume 75 per cent of the world's resources and leave the other 75 per cent of people to suffer the consequences? It is one set of people that consumes petroleum, and another set of people that are hurt by climate change. There is an ecological debt owed geographically by the countries of the north to the countries of the south. The debt is also owed historically by the white people to the indigenous people. Men owe the debt to women. Urban areas owe it to rural areas. An ecological debt is owed by our generation to future generations, and all humanity owes an ecological debt to the rest of creation.

Half of the world lives on under two dollars a day. We are afraid of terrorism and we mourn the 3000 dead in the US on September 11th, 2001. On that same day, 15,000 other people in the world were killed because of diseases related to pollution of air, water and food. Not only on September 11th, but also on September 12th, 13th and 14th and every day after that. The terrorist here is the economic system, and we have to think about that.

Canon Winkett: Dr Williams, please would you respond?

Archbishop: I want to pick up some of the things that Dr Midgley has said about religious perceptions and relate them very closely to the practical and political issues raised by Dr Navarro.

I am not completely convinced that the Christian tradition has quite such a uniformly bleak record as Dr Midgley suggests – though I would be expected to say that, of course! Christianity, like other religious traditions, sees human beings as addressed, spoken to, acted on, by God. In a great deal of the early Christian tradition there is a strong sense that the world itself is a communication, a system of meaning. It tells us how to be attuned to God. If the world speaks to humans, it follows that we are not free to impose the meanings we want onto the world. Human beings have to listen, to attune and relate to a system that doesn't depend on what is going on inside their heads.

I think this is a difficult concept for contemporary people in the Western world to accept, for all the reasons that Dr Midgley has outlined. We're afraid of being passive. We don't like being spoken to. We would rather take pre-emptive action, imposing the meanings we want on the world. The result of this, however, is that the overwhelming majority of the world's population experience meanings decided by the wealthy, by those who have access and control. A world that should speak of gift and possibility becomes a world that speaks of unequal power and oppression.

A religious person, and particularly a Christian, might want to offer a different perspective – one that first asks what the world means, what does it speak of? – not what I, as a powerful person of a certain kind, decide. The inequalities and distortions that are around in our relation to the environment are not simply immoral, they are in a real sense blasphemous – if that word has any meaning – because they are an attempt to stand in for the meanings that God imposes. This is a situation of real spiritual and political urgency. The four subjects of the dialogues are closely connected, because governance, international economics and health are all entirely bound up with this question. I would say that the ecological crisis we face makes all those other issues immeasurably more urgent.

Our challenge is to respond to this, not with impotence or passivity, but to ask locally what specific differences we can make. While there are huge questions to be addressed to the macro-political system, I hope we can also tonight focus on what specifically can be done here and now. I would be delighted to hear more from Dr Navarro about local reforestation and the ways in which communities can take on this agenda – not just as something that addresses the global crisis but, as Dr Midgley has suggested, that addresses the question of how people become properly and maturely human themselves, rather than buying into a set of adolescent fantasies about control and power.

Dr Midgley: The Christian tradition has these two sides. Certainly, the celebration of the earth as God's creation is terribly important in a great deal of Christian writing. The thought underlying these writings is that we have to take the earth seriously on its own terms, rather than turning it into anything we fancy. The other side has also had great force because it has always appealed to people who were unhappy in this life, such as the early Christians who were being persecuted and believed in the imminent end of the world. Later, people who were poor and oppressed and miserable also had this bias against the earth. Unfortunately being oppressed often makes people want power. Those same people, when given a chance, are naturally disposed to try to make the world go their own way.

Now, what I think happened at the Enlightenment is that when people thought less of the idea that God was the Creator, and were less interested in honouring him, they didn't then think, 'Oh well then, we are just part of the rest of this biosphere – let's find our place.' They thought, 'Well, who are we going to worship now? What about ourselves?' This may be putting it a bit strongly, but if there doesn't seem to be any power around and you yourself want power, there is a very great temptation to take it.

I would like to add a point about the word 'environment'. Dr Navarro, you opened your piece by saying something about our relationship to the environment, and of course that is the way we now think. I am afraid that we can make the environment sound like one of the things we ought to take an interest in, along with various arts and charities and other concerns. What the Gaia concept tells us is that there is an awful great system and we are a tiny little bit of it. It's the whole thing, not just the parts, something 'over there' that we have to consider. That means we have to think of ourselves in a quite different way.

Dr Navarro: I believe there is an inherent contradiction between how the environment works and how our economic system works. The way our economic system is set up means that it requires more and more resources. The environment, we know, has limited resources. We cannot go on in an unlimited way of behaving: it will only lead to worse and worse crises.

To answer the Archbishop's question: 'What can we do here

and now?' – there are many things that we can do. We can start with reforestation, use solar and wind energy, ride bicycles. Usually you will hear that there is not much money around. I do believe that one of the main obstacles to the sustainability of the planet is the existence of the military–industrial complex. If we stopped having armies around the world, we would have many more funds than are needed to solve the major problems facing humanity.

Inequity is another key obstacle to sustainability. We have to realise that everyone is a human being, everybody has the right to survive. Extreme poverty and extreme wealth do not support equity and they are obstacles to sustainability. I personally believe that it is very hard – not impossible but very hard – to be very wealthy and decent at the same time. As a matter of fact, it was Jesus Christ who said that it was easier for a camel to go through the eye of a needle than for a rich person to enter the Kingdom of Heaven, as we all know. Inequity has to be resolved if we want a sustainable world.

Fundamentalism is very bad – not religious fundamentalism but trade fundamentalism. You hear politicians all over the world telling you that trade is the solution. More trade needs more consumption, more oil exploitation, more carbon dioxide in the atmosphere. When I was a kid I learned to say, 'Our Father, who art in heaven …' Now the World Trade Organisation is teaching us to say, 'Our Trade, who art in heaven, hallowed be thy name …' This is what they want us to learn. So if we don't rid ourselves of trade fundamentalism we will not achieve a sustainable world.

Another obstacle to sustainability is the United States existing as a nation. It is too powerful. It should divide itself up into fifty nations as the Soviet Union did. It is such a powerful structure and its government is becoming a tool for corporations. Corporations that are interested in oil, in profits, in minerals, in diversifying, use governments. The US government is a very strong tool to be used for invasions.

We live in an economic system that is violent, an economic system that is toxic, an economic system that does not respect nature and does not respect people. Our civilisation is at stake if we do not manage to solve this inherent problem. We are heading for the same destiny as the dinosaurs and we will end up having no representatives in Gaia.

Canon Winkett: Archbishop, please would you respond to these comments and perhaps give your view on sustainable development?

Archbishop: What we have just heard is a very powerful statement of the problem that sustainability poses, given the immense political units that control a great deal of the world at the moment. I think most people find it quite hard to imagine that in the longest of long terms there can be a sustainable development that is not locally accountable. It has been one of the themes of these dialogues that there is a pervasive unease about the power blocs that we have.

It is hard to see how we can change. How do you actually sell to a political electorate the idea that their political units are too large and too ambitious, that their consumption is too high? How, in other words, do you bring the notion of limits into politics? I think that is the deepest challenge here, and it has to happen at a local level. Sustainable development is development that has a degree of accountability at the human level, small scale, and that is why it is a challenge across the board.

Canon Winkett: Would you comment on Dr Midgley's advocacy of the Gaia concept and how that might relate to Christian systems of belief?

Archbishop: My immediate reaction is to connect the language of Gaia with some of what Christian theologians across the centuries have said about Wisdom as a living reality. Some of the great Russian thinkers at the beginning of the last century regarded Wisdom as the principle of integration in the whole creation. Human beings could not act humanly unless they understood how they fitted into that integrity. For some of these writers, this did not just mean our attitude to the natural world in general, but also economics, the creative act of economics. Indeed, they saw Wisdom linking the creativity in environment, economics, art, politics and governance and holding them together. The Gaia concept echoes a great deal of what that sort of language was about.

Canon Winkett: Dr Midgley, would you comment on the Gaia philosophy of interdependence in the light of what Dr Navarro said about justice?

Dr Midgley: Everything, of course, can be linked and should be linked. It is clear that the way in which the West is systematically messing up the planet must lead to inequality and inequity among humans. Any species that messed up the resources available to it on this scale would naturally find some of its own members being in very deep trouble. I think it is as simple as that.

Is it? Am I being too simple? It seems obvious to me. One good thing about contemporary arguments on these subjects is that there isn't the gap between the people who worry about the environment and the people who worry about human injustice. Some 30 years back there was some astonishment amongst these two groups that they weren't saying the same thing. Now it is understood that these are not separate causes but a single cause. Is it imaginable that there might be a planet where there was so much of everything that it wouldn't matter how much people grabbed for themselves? No, it is not. I hope Dr Navarro thinks so too!

Archbishop: Could I just come in very briefly on that? I think part of what this brings home as well is that it is not as though we are simply facing one big ecological catastrophe. It is not a dramatic and neat and single apocalyptic event. It is the slow and appalling dissolution of peace and stability. We are facing a series of constantly spiralling local wars over water and oil. We are facing an age of collapse, a dark period.

Dr Navarro: Sustainability means the ability to sustain, but the question is, what do we want to sustain? I personally don't believe that the objective should be to sustain development. My objective is to sustain my community, my country, my region, my planet. These are what we have to sustain. Development should be a tool. If you have a boat and an engine, you need the engine in order to move the boat, but your objective is to sustain the boat. The boat is our society, the engine is our development. We need development to move, but what if we have an iceberg in front of us? What if we have climate change in front of us? We have to understand development because our misunderstanding of it has generated a great deal of trouble in the world.

To have sustainability we need four things. The textbooks say we need three things: economics, ecology and society. Of course we need to follow ecological rules such as recycling and protecting bio-diversity. We also need to respect social equity, and we must have economic rationality. But there is a fourth need, and that is good politics. We cannot have sustainability when power is concentrated in a very few hands. When power is concentrated it is hard to have social, economic or ecological justice.

Of the 100 largest economies in the world, 51 are corporations, 49 are countries. Even these countries are governed by corporate-led globalisation. Governments are giving their power to international organisations such as the WTO, and they are the ones who are deciding what is to happen in the world. Remember that in 1992 President Bush Senior didn't want to sign the Bio-diversity Convention, because 52 biological firms said he shouldn't. The present President Bush didn't go to the UN Summit on Sustainable Development in South Africa in 2002 because corporations told him not to.

We have to tell governments to take back the power that belongs to the people, and give it to them.

Archbishop: I could tie these comments back to the previous dialogue, which was about whether there was an alternative to global capitalism. One of the things I recall from that discussion was that institutions should acquire a proper power and freedom, and that large, even international institutions can be put at the service of local communities, rather than the other way round.

Electorates have to buy this. Active democracy depends upon it. It is not as if we have an existing innocent democratic world system in which a lot of people are making foolish choices. We have a world system in which people are deceived about the nature of the choices they can make. This brings us back to the question of whether sustainable development can in the long run co-exist with uncriticised, unchallenged, transnational organisations.

Dr Navarro: I believe we have to work on values – values of solidarity, for example. Solidarity doesn't mean to feel bad or to try and help the people of Chechnya, Iraq or Palestine. Solidarity means that their problems are my problems also. The destruction of nature is also my problem. It may be on the other side of the world, but it is my problem.

We were very lucky in El Salvador to have a figure like Bishop Romero, the twenty-fifth anniversary of whose killing is on 24 March 2005. The person who killed him founded a right-wing political party, and the current President of El Salvador is a member of that party, so that gives you some idea of our political system.

The idea that Bishop Romero taught us was that the social

problems facing people in El Salvador were a concern for all of us who pretended to be Christians. Being Christian was not just a matter of going to church and praying and singing. If we're serious about loving our neighbour, then the problems facing all of humanity are our problems. What is the difference between killing 3000 people in the World Trade Center in New York, and killing 15,000 people because corporations want more oil?

I believe religion plays an important role. On the twenty-fifth anniversary of Bishop Romero's death we will be planting a million trees in El Salvador. I was very happy to see Bishop Romero's statue in Westminster Abbey earlier today, and I would invite all of you to plant trees here in the UK in memory of Bishop Romero.

Dr Midgley: A word about the word 'development'. When one talks about sustainable development, one cannot, I think, mean development in the sense in which it is so often taken now, which is simply the expansion of industry and of the complicated, expensive way of life that we have developed through our industries. The phrase 'sustainable development' is ambiguous. That anything should be sustainable must mean that it can and should go on. Development, in the sense of something going on and on growing, cannot. Take plants and animals as a metaphor. Plants and animals develop but only to a point. It has not been noticed enough that they stop. A horse doesn't go on growing forever. There is that within almost all organisms that says 'Stop growing' at a certain point. I believe crocodiles keep it up a bit too long! But usually the growth and development of organisms is finite. It's perfectly clear, since our resources on this planet are limited, that this stopping principle also needs to be applied to economic growth. It wouldn't hurt if we remarked upon this strange metaphor of development more. We are the 'developed world', aren't we? It's not a very sensible thought.

Archbishop: An idea that surfaced in the first of our dialogues was that the world could eventually be harmonised by means of universal accessibility of better information technology systems. This idea begs rather a lot of questions in precisely the ways that have been outlined here. I wonder whether others would agree that there is something about the language of information technology that suggests an impatience with the very medium of communication? The language betrays an impatience of time taking – that is to say, an impatience with the body. Virtual reality is very attractive because bodily limitation is bracketed out for that time. There is a Messianism around this that undermines the sense of what we actually, concretely are: part of the physical system. Virtual reality rests on what seems to me to be a fantasy view of the resources that can be devoted to it.

Dr Midgley: There is nothing new in this. People have always taken refuge in words when realities are too complicated and frightening. This enormous expansion of communication, however, makes it easier and more widespread. I saw a report last week about a computer game in which you can have a virtual girlfriend or boyfriend, who of course is going to give you much less trouble than the ordinary kind. You can buy them presents, and then they treat you better. The money involved is real: you pay money to play this game. Somehow, though, you receive a substitute for the disturbing realities. It seems to me that a lot of the communication revolution is roughly about avoidance. It serves to extend fantasy. Now, I know that there are absolutely splendid uses for information technology. Computers have made things possible in science that wouldn't otherwise have been possible. They are excellent *tools*. My husband was a computer wizard. He used to get very cross when people referred to computers as intelligent machines. 'They are not intelligent,' he'd say. 'They are dumb, they are stupid, you have no idea how stupid they are. They are tools which have to be used.' Now, I don't think we have got any better at deciding what to do with our technology, and I don't share the optimism that it sometimes generates. It could be used to do jobs of the utmost importance, but will it?

Dr Navarro: Communication is certainly very important. It is, however, also ideological. The problem is that the communication we have, by and large, by the normal media, is the information that keeps the system going. There is no political will from those who have the power to solve the major problems facing humanity – basic problems such as lack of water and sanitation. We know how to solve these basic problems but instead we spend one million million dollars every year on the military industry, because it benefits some corporations. Technology can be useful but the benefits are limited as long as there is no political will to solve the problems we are facing. If you look at what is being communicated through education and even some religions, it is often supporting the *status quo.*

If I call myself a Christian, I should question the economic system that we have. I should question our negligence. I should not try just to make small changes that make people feel a little better. I should be radical, reach back to the roots, which is the Latin source of the word 'radical'. To be radical is not to be violent. Jesus Christ was one of the most radical guys when he told us, 'You are here with me, or you are not with me.' Not Bush, who also said that. Christ. Martin Luther King was another very radical person, and so was Mahatma Gandhi, who was also a very peaceful one. Even the word 'radical' has been hijacked, as if the word meant 'violent'. It does not. Radical changes in the mentality of people is what we need.

Canon Winkett: Could I put the first question from the floor: 'What can the churches do to help the ecological crisis?'

Archbishop: A brief answer: churches need to look at their own operations and audit them. It is no good the churches raising the issue – they have to set an example as well. Eco-congregation has been an important element of this already. Then the churches can give their backing to certain specific projects, such as Contraction and Convergence. This is an international movement asking the governments of the world to agree to contract the amount of greenhouse gases going into the atmosphere to a level the earth can bear, and sharing out the right to emit gases on a per-head-of-population basis. Those richer countries where the emissions far outweigh the number of people should pay for their surplus and the payment go to those countries where the emissions are much less but the populations much greater, namely the developing world.

The churches can back something like Contraction and Convergence publicly and unanimously because, at its core, it is just. There are opportunities to push this agenda forward, such as the British presidency of G8 in 2005.

Dr Navarro: I believe churches have to work at values. They have to find the social and ecological dimension of religious values. For example, what does 'love your neighbour' mean socially and ecologically? The churches must confront people and corporations with reality. The churches should not just pray, though that is very important too. They should ask themselves what it means to be a Christian in a world where thousands and thousands of people are being destroyed by industry, ecological deterioration, wars, and social poverty.

Canon Winkett: The second question from the floor is, 'To what extent does a democratic government inhibit the radical and unpopular measures we need to reduce climate change?' Dr Navarro.

Dr Navarro: I would like to ask, which country is a democratic one? People in the United States, where I have lived, believe they have a democratic country because sometimes they have

Republicans and sometimes they have Democrats. The difference is that Republicans are supported by Pepsi Cola, and the Democrats by Coca Cola. There is no real change. I believe we need democracy, but democracy means power to the people, not power to the politicians, much less the corporations.

Dr Midgley: I don't think it can be right to suggest that democracy inhibits taking measures to reduce climate change, because if that were so, we would see some undemocratic governments that were getting it right, wouldn't we? I don't see dictatorships around the world that have a very good environmental policy.

The trouble with both kinds of governments is that there are very strong vested interests in keeping things as they are. As Churchill said about democracy, 'It's not the best kind of government but it's a great deal better than anything else.' Since we live in what is supposed to be a democracy, we are very conscious of the obstacles that confront us here. They are very real and terrible.

We should look at history. If you had been living in the 1840s and you had wanted to do something about the workers' conditions in factories, you would have despaired. Not only was every vested interest supporting this appalling system, but the economic theorists said that it was necessary. It was people such as John Stuart Mill and Shaftesbury and others who pulled on their boots and tried to do something. By their efforts came the Factory Acts and other measures to ameliorate the system. Our predecessors fought these systems. We haven't had to fight them lately but it is time we did. Without these earlier fights, we wouldn't have all the institutions of which we approve. In the United States, for example, National Parks were created by Theodore Roosevelt and other unsavoury characters got up and shouted and made a nuisance of themselves until they got the National Parks. That is how change happens. I don't see how we can possibly say that it is our system of government that makes it hard to introduce necessary changes.

Archbishop: It is true, as has been said, that we have some illusions about the degree of democracy that we enjoy. That won't do for an alibi, however. The issue is about the real, demonstrable need for sustainability, not just of one country's population, but of the whole human race. I suspect that in the next decade there will be some very hard choices facing a number of governments about controlling and limiting development. I hope that churches, other bodies, NGOs, which are clearly aware of the real long-term interests of us all, will keep sustainability clearly and sufficiently in the sphere of public discourse. I hope these groups will assist – let's be bold – assist any government that is prepared to take a risk and move towards certain limitations and penalties to enforce them. I see this happening in the next decade. It's unavoidable.

Canon Winkett: Another questioner asks, 'Does the Christian attitude towards the nature of stewardship not contradict Gaia and the belief that humans and nature are equal?'

Dr Midgley: Yes, it is a criticism that those who propound the concept of Gaia have made all along, that the notion of stewardship is too patronising. Of course, 'stewardship' is a great deal better than 'uncontrolled rapacity'. Stewardship has much to be said for it, but it does presuppose that we know a lot better what is required in nature than nature itself does. It assumes that humans can choose the aims that nature can put before itself.

The Christian people who talked about stewardship were not wrong. On its terms, humans should know their responsibility is to God, and as the Archbishop pointed out, God really was supposed to have known what he was about when he created all this stuff. If there were lots and lots of trees, this was not to be taken to be just a mistake. The notion of stewardship is lost when you take yourself to be the owner.

Change of imagery really is quite important. The imagery of

Gaia takes us back to the way the Greeks thought. They called the earth Gaia – that is, the mother of gods and men. It seemed to them a very natural way to think. Out of the earth came all the things that they valued, themselves and everything else. Gaia was not taken to be one of the Olympian gods who had social goings-on in Homer. They didn't tell silly stories about her. They did, however, continue to revere her. To use that word is to put ourselves back into a situation where to revere the earth seems natural. This is not to suggest that we should now say 'Gaia' instead of 'God' and invent a new religion. It's a change of perspective, a change in the way we see our own relation to the whole. Once you do that, you don't feel so keen to call yourself a steward.

Archbishop: The question is interesting, not least in its phraseology. The phrase about the equality of humans and nature begs a question itself. It is not as if there is one thing called nature and something quite other called humanity. In Christian theology there is a creation in which human beings have a unique role, as does every other bit of creation. Now the uniqueness of the human role and calling within creation is something that has been variously expressed. Sometimes it is expressed in such a way that the rest of the system is downgraded. I would like to throw another concept into the discussion, in addition to stewardship, one that you find a bit in the Greek tradition and also in our own poetic tradition. That is the concept of priesthood. Humanity has a priestly role in nature, a calling to make explicit and visible the meanings that are there in creation, to hold them up for understanding and contemplation, and to make sense of the world – God's sense, that is, not their own. The priestly role also calls us to exercise a ministry of reconciliation.

This role allows both for the inseparable involvement of humanity in the rest of creation, and also recognises that there is something about humans that other creatures don't have, just as there are some things that creatures have and humans don't have. The particularly human calling to act as a priest is deeply ingrained in the Wisdom tradition, in Hebrew Scripture and in the Christian tradition.

Canon Winkett: Another question is, 'Can small-scale projects really assist in avoiding cataclysm?'

Dr Navarro: It depends on the projects. Things like bicycles have a very important place on earth. Technology has to be appropriate for the local social and ecological conditions. The problem is that we have technologies that are mass-produced and then distributed everywhere, including many places where they are not appropriate. When you transfer technology, you transfer the social and economic conditions that made the technology possible in the first place. Sometimes these do not apply.

Archbishop: I am glad to hear the reference to appropriate technology. I think that the economic and technical assumptions that we have come to make in the North Atlantic world are regularly taken to be the ones that are natural for human beings everywhere. We assume everyone wants these things. This is nonsense. People are certainly educated into wanting these things through information technology that spreads unreal aspiration. But justice requires us to stop taking for granted that our models and scales of thinking are appropriate everywhere. Equally we should challenge their appropriateness in our own setting. We are back with the question of development and its limits.

On the general principle that it is better to light a candle than to curse the darkness, I think that wherever you are, do something. That something is a testimony that it is possible to do things differently, and that testimony is what changes the values, the perceptions, the myths we live by – if I may quote the title of a book I very much enjoyed.

Canon Winkett: Could the panel say more about the use of imagination in approaching ecological issues? Connected with this, I'll ask this additional question: 'As we become an increasingly urban species, how do we connect with the natural world?'

Dr Midgley: This is terribly important and there is no single way of dealing with it. I have said a bit already about how our way of feeling and imagining is crucial to what we think. It's a great mistake to suppose that what we think is science and factual, and we have our feelings about the facts afterwards. The attitude that we have determines the questions we ask, and, therefore, determines a great deal of the answer.

When I was at school in the country I used to go out in the winter nights and look at the stars for a long time. Not for any sort of study – I just wanted to see this very vast pattern out there, and think about how far away they might be. You can't do that now and that is a real deprivation.

We must, however, use the light we do have. When we find ourselves using machine metaphors all the time as if people were machines, or bits of people were machines, we should question ourselves. So much of the constantly burgeoning rhetoric is pointless and misleading. We have to watch out for the bits that are right.

I don't think that the fact that many people are now brought up in towns prevents this, but it does make it harder. We must guard against strengthening this narrowness. I don't want to give unkind examples, but – oh dear! – I was looking at an article in a paper today which said how terribly important fashion is, and how mistaken you would be if you thought it was trivial and trifling. The writer wasn't being totally silly. She was talking about how important our self-image is to us. I do think, though, that journalists could choose to write articles differently. In our conversation we are constantly using imaginative patterns and making a difference to how others use them. We simply must not take the inevitability of how things are going for granted. We must look out for the opportunity to make important changes.

Archbishop: Are we seeing a need for a new asceticism? I don't mean simply giving things up and downsizing our lifestyle, though those are important in their way. I mean a deliberate policy of engaging with the limits of the natural world – walking more, getting wet, digging gardens, very simple things. It does seem to me that there is a proper asceticism about that, about getting your hands on the reality of the world and recognising in that engagement that there is a limit to what you can actually do as a body in a material world. It is good for you to face that limit. Go for a walk in the rain – you know, basic asceticism.

Dr Midgley: Even things which aren't out of doors that may show you your limits are pretty healthy.

Canon Winkett: The final question is, 'Is nuclear power the solution to the problem of global warming?'

Dr Navarro: I don't believe so. The intention behind nuclear power is to provide energy to big, demanding centres. Do they really need the energy? Couldn't we develop solar power? If you have a good solar collector you don't need to pay every time you get the sun. Nuclear power is technology concentrated in a very few hands, and that means profit to them alone. Governments subsidise research on nuclear power. Why do they not subsidise research on wind power, for example? Or solar energy? I don't believe that nuclear power should be part of the response to the energy demands in the world.

Archbishop: I'm not sure. I think it is, as Dr Navarro has said, a question of scale. If we are looking at sustaining a large-scale economic enterprise, there is a case for saying that nuclear power is preferable, because it is less poisonous than fossil fuels. We must, however, keep the question of size in view.

Historically, of course, the attraction of nuclear power as an area of research has something to do with the fact that there are other, less savoury uses for nuclear research. So I'm undecided. I see the problem, and if it is a choice between the constant search for more pollutant fossil fuel sources and nuclear power, then there is a case, but I don't think I can be firmer than that.

Dr Midgley: I think the Archbishop is right. If one was omnipotent one might say at the moment that you must try everything. You must try all the renewable sources of energy as hard as you can; economise on what you are currently using, because it is grossly excessive; but we might also say that we need some nuclear as well. The trouble with this option is the political repercussions. Many countries greatly desire nuclear weapons because possessing them forces other countries to take them seriously. This is disastrous. Those countries that do have nuclear weapons should give them up. Countries have been working towards this but not far and fast enough. Nuclear power certainly cannot be thought of as a solution.

Canon Winkett: Could I ask each of you to sum up your response to the question of the relationship between humanity and the environment?

Dr Midgley: They must be seen as part of the same problem. Those who work on environment, and those who work on development, must not quarrel with each other.

Dr Navarro: We and the rest of nature are just one life. All people, all over the world, and all species, are all living. The Creator, when he or she made it, made some rules that we are not now respecting. What we have as our development, our civilisation, is contrary to the way Gaia works. If we want a planet that is sustainable, we have to make radical changes. Our economic system is not proper for life.

Archbishop: First, I should like to offer the fundamental perception, necessary and central to a religious vision, that the world is a gift. It is alive with meaningful and loving communication. Rejection and distortion of that loving communication is blasphemous. Second, I want to say something about freedom. We are all imprisoned to a greater or lesser extent by the notion of freedom as infinite possibilities of choice, but the freedom of suicide is not a very good model for freedom. Freedom to be what we are in a world which has limits, rhythms and connections, is the freedom that we should hold in the centre of our vision.

Canon Winkett: It remains to me to thank you all for coming tonight, for your attentiveness and for your excellent questions. Thank you to our panel. Good night.

Chapter Four
Is Humanity Killing Itself?

 *The fourth St Paul's Institute dialogue was held at St Paul's Cathedral on 30 September 2004 between Dr Rowan Williams, Archbishop of Canterbury, Dr Ian Smith and Mr Peter Bains. It was chaired by Dame Elizabeth Butler-Sloss, head of the Family Division of the High Court and a member of the Court of Appeal at the Royal Courts of Justice. She has ruled on many of the most morally complex and controversial cases of our times.*

Dame Butler-Sloss: Good evening and welcome to St Paul's Cathedral. Our two interlocutors tonight come from the worlds of public and commercial medicine. Dr Ian Smith spent ten years as a medical missionary in a hospital in a very remote part of Nepal, and six years in Kathmandu with the national tuberculosis programme. He has two adoptive children, who are both Nepalese. His wife is a nurse and works with him. He is now the Adviser to the Director General of the World Health Organisation. He has been managing the Global TB Drug Facility, which makes grants of drugs to treat almost two million TB patients in 48 countries.

Mr Peter Bains is the Senior Vice President of International Commercial Development at Glaxo SmithKline. He is Industry Chair of the Accelerating Access initiative, which is a United Nations and pharmaceutical industry partnership in the global fight against HIV/AIDS. He works closely with the WHO.

Could I ask you both to give us your opening statement on tonight's subject?

Dr Smith: Thank you very much and good evening, everybody. The question posed in the title – 'Is Humanity Killing Itself?' – is a provocative one. Clearly, humans have the capacity to do so and, at times, apparently the intent. If you were to compare the costs on expenditures on military aid, for example, with overseas development assistance for health, it would become clear where human priorities lie. But I would argue that the weapons of mass destruction that threaten health are not simply armaments. They include poverty, inequity, unbridled consumerism and environmental degradation.

From the point of view of public health, there are at least four reasons to fear the future. First there is the threat of a major disease pandemic. Recently a mother and her child died of Avian Influenza in Thailand. Their deaths raise the spectre of a global 'flu pandemic. The second threat is of biological warfare. The anthrax scare in the United States three years ago drew attention to the way that disease itself can be used deliberately to kill many people. Thirdly, there is a potential threat of technology taking humanity in dangerous directions – for example, through human reproductive cloning. Finally, there is a threat of a growing elderly population that cannot look after itself.

If I were to ask the question, 'Is humanity killing itself?' of my colleagues in Nepal, I think I would hear a very different answer from the one I might give. People living in poverty rarely have the luxury of even thinking about the future. For them the present is fearful enough. Let me illustrate what I mean. There have been profound improvements in health over the last century. Over the last 50 years we have seen the global average life expectancy increase by nearly two decades from 46 years in 1950 to 65 years in 2002. This statistic, however, hides huge gaps and disparities in different parts of the world. The life expectancy for women in developed countries is 78, while for men in sub-Saharan Africa it is 46. In some parts of Africa, death rates are higher than they were 30 years ago. Forty million people are living with HIV. Six million of them need treatment with anti-retrovirals, but only 440,000 people are receiving them. HIV is rapidly becoming a disease of young women. Two thirds of those aged 15 to 24 living with HIV are female. Each year, about 57 million people die around the world from any cause. About 10.5 million of those who die are children, the vast majority of them in the poorest countries. About nine million of those childhood deaths are preventable.

Awareness of the profound effect of inequity on illness is not new. The WHO and many of the UN agencies were created after the Second World War in order to protect future genera-tions, and the constitution of the WHO recognises health as a human right. It acknowledges the role that equity, government responsibility and community participation all play in pro-moting and protecting health. More recently, the Millennium summit set specific development goals to reduce poverty by half by the year 2015. Of the eight 'Millennium Development Goals' that were announced, three were directly related to health: reducing maternal mortality; reducing childhood deaths; and reducing the spread of communicable diseases such as TB, HIV and malaria.

A couple of years ago the economist Jeffrey Sachs coined the term 'weapons of mass salvation' to describe a series of highly effective inventions against HIV, TB, malaria and other com-mon conditions affecting the poor of the world. To me it was highly appropriate that he made the biblical link between salvation and health. My answer to the question, 'Is humanity killing itself?', then, is 'Not all of it, but certainly the poorest parts.'

Mr Bains: Thank you, Dame Elizabeth, and good evening. Is humanity killing itself? The more I considered this question, the more profound and the more polarised it became in my mind. There are macro-indicators that appear to paint a positive and optimistic picture. The global population has doubled from three billion in 1960 to over six billion today. Global life expectancy has increased by almost 20 years over a 50-year period. Global childhood survival rates have improved to their highest level yet of 92 per cent. In 1970 they were only 85 per cent.

Beyond these headline statistics, however, lie deeply disturbing threats and realities. Two of the most disturbing global threats relate to the potential catastrophic risk of climate change and environmental degradation through the abuse and over-use of the earth's eco-systems. There are the unthinkable consequences of the use of weapons of mass destruction: our capacity to kill the global population already exists many times over. I should like to focus on the dreadful realities behind the headline health indicators, however. The roots of avoidable disease and death lie in poverty and the widening inequality gap between the developed and the developing worlds. As Dr Smith has said, while global life expectancy has improved, in parts of Africa it has declined by 20 years to levels below those of 30 years ago. There are many more statistics to show the health inequalities between rich and poor countries. Life expectancy in Japan has reached over 85 years, whereas in Sierra Leone it is less than half that, at 36 years. Of the 10.5 million children who died before the age of five in 1992, 98 per cent of those were in the developing world, and 19 of the 20 worst-affected countries were in Africa. In Finland and Iceland childhood mortality rates are less than 4 per cent. In Sierra Leone they are over 30 per cent.

Millions of lives are being lost prematurely to infectious diseases due to lack of access to even basic health-care systems, infrastructures and medicine. The spectre of HIV/AIDS has loomed over the astonishingly short period of 20 years to become the leading cause of infectious death worldwide in adults aged 15 to 59, and now accounts for a staggering 1 in 20 of all deaths worldwide. The scale of the HIV pandemic is drastic and deeply disturbing, and a sobering portent of new viral diseases that could become prevalent, especially to vulnerable populations.

The world is fighting back, however, including the pharmaceutical industry. Glaxo SmithKline's response to the crisis has not been perfect as, along with many stakeholders, we were taken by surprise at the speed, scale and scope of the AIDS pandemic. Now, however, we are contributing to the fight-back. The most important contribution that the pharmaceutical industry can make to global pandemics is research and development that will provide the new treatments and vaccines. We should not forget the limits of current anti-retroviral treatment. We still have no cure and no vaccine for AIDS. The industry can also contribute to making drugs affordable. Glaxo SmithKline has offered its vaccines at preferential prices for over 20 years and for HIV medicines since 1997. Our anti-retrovirals are now available at 'not for profit' prices in over 100 of the world's poorest countries.

We fund community-led HIV initiatives in over 100 countries where we operate. We are a key partner in the WHO's Global Programme to eliminate lymphatic filariasis. We will donate about six billion tablets over the 20-year life of that programme. Third, the industry can help with improving access to medicines, and we continue to look for new ways to do this. These include granting voluntary licences to generic companies so that they too can manufacture unbranded anti-retrovirals, increasing availability to people with HIV/AIDS. This sort of response to the crisis is not only right, but it also makes good business sense. Our shareholders agree with us that saving lives and making profits are not mutually exclusive. Glaxo SmithKline is passionate about the role it is playing alongside other stakeholders.

The WHO has set the ambitious target of 'three by five' – treating three million people with HIV in developing countries by the year 2005. This goal will not be achieved without significant funding, which must be maintained over the long term. More can be and must be done by governments, the public sector and the private sector to prevent the HIV tragedy from expanding and to bring it under control. Although welcome resources are coming through, funding remains inadequate. Wealthy countries must commit more.

In conclusion, the answer to the question, 'Is humanity killing itself?' is in the balance. While some indicators appear positive, impending threats of devastating consequence remain, and there exists an unacceptably high level of unnecessary death and suffering. Technological advances mean we are living in a time of unprecedented opportunity for health. For all humanity to reap the benefits, the global community must provide the political will, additional resources and a spirit of partnership. Glaxo SmithKline is committed to improving its initiatives, learning lessons and looking for further opportunities for the future. All global stakeholders must play their part to the full.

Dame Butler-Sloss: Dr Williams, would you respond?

Archbishop: The bleak view that we have heard is persuasive. We have learned that the developed world is at risk of killing itself by over-consumption and mismanagement of the environment, and indirectly killing the rest of the world by sustaining systems of poverty and inequity. That is the bottom line from both presentations. I find myself asking some different questions, and I should like to hear your views on them.

The first question is to do with relating health and spirit. Health is, of course, not just a physical phenomenon. It is an attunement to and at-homeness in the world at large. It is an inner and an outer, a spiritual and a physical reality. If I am right in saying this, then threats to health are also threats to the human soul. Campaigns to promote health are, then, inevitably bound up with a commitment to intensifying the right kind of self-belief and the right kind of harmonious relationships that go with that. Poverty, as we all know, affects both mind and body – spirit and body. This is why one of the interesting developments in thinking about health care generally here in the UK, and worldwide in recent years, has been the recovery of a sense of ownership or control. Health care has come to mean equipping people to take responsibility for their own health and for their community's health. Health care does not now just mean providing a cure, but also nourishing a spirit of self-trust, creativity and responsibility.

This linking of health and spirit relates to a political question. If we think about health and democracy, it is in the long run impossible to see one flourishing without the other. A fully democratic society is one in which people take confident responsibility for their own conditions, and it is also one in which power is shared and understood as shared.

If health, spirit and full democracy are all linked, then there need to be appropriate incentives for partnerships between governments, commerce and community enterprise. This issue has already crossed the radar of people in government in this country. For example, there are schemes for proper graded incentives to keep down the price of drugs to assist pharmaceutical companies to do the job that they are there for. Pharmaceutical companies cannot be expected absolutely to cease operating as commercial units and do a social-welfare job. There has to be public incentive, encouragement and partnership. Constructing these is a major practical challenge for government, voluntary organisations, and the industry itself.

Dame Butler-Sloss: Dr Smith, would you like to comment?

Dr Smith: Yes, thank you for those very interesting questions. I would strongly support the idea of a fully democratic society with people taking confident responsibility for their own health. If we lived in a world in which information was rational and available to all and people's judgements were based on that rational information, such a vision would be realisable. But we don't live in such a world. In our world we are pressured to conform to certain social standards and behaviours. In a consumer society, those pressures come from the people who market particular ways of life. WHO has argued in many parts of the world for healthier diets and life-styles, and the response is that it is not up to governments to pressure people to adopt healthy lifestyles, it's up to individual choice. That would be acceptable if people had equal access to proper information about what a healthy life-style was. But they don't, and so in practice your vision does not work.

Archbishop: I absolutely recognise where we are. I'm not suggesting we can create a healthy democracy overnight. Rather, I want to suggest that the dissemination of your rational information is the priority and that everywhere we can we work towards that. That requires a lot of individuals choosing not to put the right to individual choice at the top of their list of priorities!

Mr Bains: I agree with Dr Smith. In the poorer parts of the world where we work, there is simply not the infrastructure and capacity for your wonderful vision of full democracy. It will remain a dream until there is political will at the level of government, nation and amongst stakeholders.

Dame Butler-Sloss: Could we pick up on the point made by Dr Williams about a sense of ownership and control within one's local community? Work could begin on a small scale more effectively than galvanising large numbers of people all at once.

Dr Smith: My initial work in Nepal was managing a community health and development programme that had the aim of building community capacity and ownership of health and education institutions. I remain firmly committed to that kind of local capacity building. We can't treat these communities in isolation, though, because they all operate within a political context that has its effect. A sense of community ownership and responsibility is fundamental to health, but so often the environment within which people are living denies them that opportunity.

The WHO constitution makes the point very clearly that the sense of participation is vital for health. Health is not just the absence of disease and infirmity – it is a state of physical, mental and social well-being. I understand that the founding fathers of WHO did consider adding the word 'spiritual' at that point.

Archbishop: Are you saying that a properly working community health development programme could in fact have a broader political impact? That implies that, as a community programme develops, it will move people into accepting a wider responsibility for the wider context.

Mr Bains: I think it can. Community projects have a very important role to play. If we look at what is happening today in Africa, the success stories are where the community projects are. Awareness raising, education, training and a sense of hope and responsibility evolve within these projects. Unfortunately they tend to be isolated pilot projects within vast seas that have to be navigated. But they do represent models that can be replicated, not least in their scale.

Archbishop: The words 'political will' have been used in every one of the dialogues. How do we develop the political will *here*? How do we assist and support the government in creating incentives for partnerships that will effect change?

Dr Smith: I think there has been real change in the way society has started to address some of these major global issues. Take the case of treating tuberculosis, which was my own area of work. It became clear during the last 20 years that although we were doing reasonably well in providing treatment for people, the treatment lasted too long – eight to twelve months – and people were not completing the drug regime. As a result they were not being cured. At that time there was no real incentive for the pharmaceutical industry to get involved in developing appropriate drugs with shorter regimes, because eight million people a year, mostly in developing countries, did not amount to much of a market. So we consulted with the industry over a two- or three-year period and developed some approaches to bring together the public-health needs of appropriate medicine with the corporate role of research and development. We worked hard to identify problems and overcome them. These types of partnerships have multiplied over recent years, in drugs, vaccines and diagnostics, in TB, malaria and HIV. The partnerships fructify when each organisation maintains its individual role and responsibility but all of us work towards a common goal.

Mr Bains: I would echo and amplify what Dr Smith has said. There is a recognition that very unique health-care challenges require non-traditional and unique responses. There is plenty of room for public–private partnerships – indeed, they are essential. We must pull together the resources and capabilities of public and private enterprises to address the disparities and inequalities of resource-poor settings.

Political will is fundamental to this. It is being mobilised in some areas – for example, in the fights against HIV/AIDS, malaria and TB, with global funds being set up for these purposes. But the scale of the political initiatives is still insufficient. The scale needs to be the same as for military budgeting if any difference is to be made.

Dr Smith: I think there is considerable political will expressed in words but not enough is translated into action. For example, at the Monterey Conference on sustainable development in 2002, commitments were made by countries with major economies to contribute 0.7 per cent of gross domestic product to overseas development. Only four countries have so far honoured that commitment. In the UK there is an International Financing Facility that should accelerate progress towards the promised 0.7 per cent, but we do have to hold fast to the commitment to turn words into action.

Archbishop: The International Finance Facility has to be enforced! But that points up yet another recurring theme in these dialogues, which is the difficulty nations have in pooling their sovereignty, to put it neutrally, to deal with issues that are not confined to national boundaries. One urgent example is in the lack of water resources, which will be a major threat to global stability in the next couple of decades. To deal with this, there is a need not only for the water itself, but also for inter-governmental, cross-boundary checks on accessibility and cleanliness, for a start. Political will has to break through a glass frontier for effective action to take place.

Dame Butler-Sloss: How far do you see this as a problem in the work that you're doing, Dr Smith?

Dr Smith: I'm not qualified to speak on the issue of water specifi-cally, but I can relate it to the threat of Avian 'Flu. Any response to a potential global pandemic clearly goes beyond any single country's borders, and it is clearly in the global interest to control such outbreaks. Because of this, there are talks going on now amongst WHO's member states to develop International Health Regulations. These are designed, first of all, to develop appropriate responses to any outbreak, including investigating it. Immediately, issues of sovereignty arise. First, a country has to be trusted to report an outbreak of a disease of global significance. Any country that does that is likely to see an instant and profound impact on trade and travel. Such issues as these have to be dealt with on an inter-governmental basis because there is no place in the world for a nation to go it alone.

Dame Butler-Sloss: Mr Bains, how does it affect your work?

Mr Bains: Profoundly. HIV is a virus, and viruses do not respect sovereign boundaries. They cross them with impunity. Take the example of SARS, which was traced to a lift in a hotel in Hong Kong, and travelled to Canada. So inter-governmental co-operation is vital to control diseases. By coming together, governments can learn from each other and build on best practice.

Archbishop: Could I move us to a different area, of interest at national and international levels and a challenge to industry? That is the question of research priorities. Where do you look for real urgencies? What dictates your search? Is it reactive? Does it attempt to look forward? Is it dictated by population size and local market size? What are the moral considerations?

Dame Butler-Sloss: Mr Bains?

Mr Bains: All the questions you list are included in any research assessment exercise. The priorities are set by finding unmet medical needs, and – of course, speaking from the perspective of a private company – returning investment to our share-holders. Alzheimer's disease is an example of an unmet medical need with grave morbidity and mortality. We don't turn a blind eye to the diseases of the developing world, however. Our company has dedicated resources to conduct research and development into these exclusively. Our targeted priorities are HIV/AIDS, malaria and TB, as I mentioned previously.

Dame Butler-Sloss: Dr Smith, what is your perspective on that?

Dr Smith: People often speak of the 10/90 gap: about 90 per cent of resources in research are spent on 10 per cent of the global population. Mr Bains' response was a good one, however. There is a lot of work going on now to shift the research agenda to more appropriate fields so as to respond to the global burden of disease, not just the rich burden. But this is not just the responsibility of industry, it is also the responsibility of government. A great deal of primary research is funded by the public sector through universities and national institutes. The research agenda is set there too, and it too needs to address ways of creating a healthier world.

Archbishop: That's why I imagined it will be a familiar issue to our audience. The question of where resources go in an under-resourced area makes for tragic choices even for a local hospital. When we cannot respond with full effectiveness to every need there is, decisions have to be taken. This is where the democracy question comes in again. Decisions may be taken on the basis of what builds a community's health, and perhaps they should be taken with that in mind. But that leaves out the specialist illnesses. Do we sacrifice the individual who may suffer from a rare condition for the sake of the community, when there is not enough for both to be cared for? There are real moral collisions here.

Dr Smith: I agree, but I would issue a warning from history. In the eighties and nineties, those from neo-liberal economies were arguing for cost-effective approaches to our major social issues, including health. It was assumed that the pot is of a fixed size and therefore we had to ration what was in that pot. We have moved on from there. The pot isn't of a fixed size. If health is truly a right, then it is something we should aspire towards and we should not limit the pot and make choices within it. We should be expanding the pot!

Archbishop: I accept the corrective. Too much of the discussion can be dominated by a model of basic scarcity, as if it was a law of nature that there is only so much on offer. That does bring us back to political will, however. There has to be an acceptance that health is not a minority concern, but something that affects the flourishing of the entire society.

Dame Butler-Sloss: So where do we go from here, Dr Williams?

Archbishop: Could I throw a spanner in the works? I would like to hear your views about alternative therapies and the use of traditional remedies in different cultural settings. Are these ever factored in to WHO programmes or to the pharmaceutical industry's work?

Mr Bains: That is definitely a spanner in the works as far as I am concerned! My personal view is that some alternative and traditional medicines in some countries clearly have therapeutic effects. These are not documented in a way that I, as a representative of the Western research-based industry, would want it, in the form of clinical trials data. Nevertheless, I do think that there is room for good traditional medicine and Western medicine to work in an integrated and holistic manner. I would exclude quackery from that partnership – there is a lot of quackery in the developing world markets.

Dame Butler-Sloss: As a doctor, Dr Smith, how do you see it?

Dr Smith: You may be surprised to hear this, but I respond very positively to alternative medicine when there is evidence that it works. Digitalis is a mainstay of the treatment of heart disease. It is derived from foxgloves, and it was widely used before people were aware of what the compound was that was helping cure people. More recently, a new product called Artemisinin, from a plant grown in China, is now the mainstay of treatment for malaria. But it has been used on malaria in China for centuries. These are two examples where traditional medicine has made a major contribution to health care in the future. There are also a lot of so-called alternative therapies for which the evidence is a lot weaker. The position of WHO has always been to use it if it works and can be proved to work.

Archbishop: One reason for raising the issue was to take us right back to an earlier stage in the conversation when we were talking about taking local resources seriously rather than simply importing alien products. I'm glad you both mentioned the problem of quackery. One of the appalling effects of the HIV pandemic in sub-Saharan Africa, especially southern Africa, has been the burgeoning of not just ineffective but unbelievably damaging and destructive 'therapies'.

Dame Butler-Sloss: Is that dealt with through education, do you think?

Archbishop: It certainly is a question of education. It's a question of offering that rational information we mentioned right at the beginning. It is difficult to offer this in a situation where there is a mixture of fatalism, mistrust of the Westernised professional and desperation.

Dr Smith: It is obviously an issue of culture. When we were in Nepal, I remember very clearly one particular episode in which I was called to treat a child of one of the staff of an international

NGO working in the same town as us. When I got there, the traditional medicine man was also doing his rites for the child. Clearly, the family had thought they should try everything. I think, for many people, when they are in a desperate position and there is little hope, they grasp at every straw.

Dame Butler-Sloss: Was there any incompatibility between what you were going to prescribe and what the medicine man prescribed?

Dr Smith: Not in that particular instance, but in other instances, yes.

Dame Butler-Sloss: Could I put the first question from the floor: 'Is global population growth itself the biggest threat to the survival of humanity?'

Mr Bains: If you extrapolate human population growth on a geometric basis with no end, the environment clearly becomes a rate-limiting factor, as it won't be able to cope. The prominent threats to humanity are a consequence not only of numbers of people but also of the industrialism around people that is damaging the environment.

Dr Smith: I would agree. Population growth was a strong argument 10 or 20 years ago, when we all felt there wasn't enough food to go around. Now we know we can feed the world, but the food is in the wrong place. Compare Japan, which can sustain a high density of population, with other, very poor countries unable to sustain even very low densities of population. The threat is not simply population growth. It is far more complex than that.

Archbishop: Thinking has moved on decisively in the last 20 or 30 years. I certainly grew up hearing this mantra that we can't feed the population of the world. Clearly, an indefinitely extrapolated population growth is going to be dangerous, but that's not what we face at the moment. We're actually aware of declining populations in the developed world. We have to factor in issues around density, urbanisation, problems such as those we see in the *favela* in Latin America and their equivalent in other countries. These are the places where population growth becomes a major health problem, because of factors which are not themselves to do with health or population growth as such. Location, density and management of population growth and movement are complex issues.

Dame Butler-Sloss: The next question: 'Is the West killing humanity?'

Archbishop: You know, at the moment I suspect it probably is, for all the reasons that we have heard to do with our rate of consumption and pollution – not as a Western phenomenon but as a Western-originated phenomenon. That is why I said the developed world kills itself by its own over-consumption. The growing health problems that develop in prosperous populations create and sustain an unjust international order. There are responses to this and things that can be done about it. It is becoming ever more urgent.

Mr Bains: You could argue that the burden of responsibility for preventable deaths may lie disproportionately on the West. I think the West does have a responsibility to provide the resources for preventable deaths in resource-poor settings. This is part of the earlier discussion about the global political will to deal with this, because the problems are beyond the capability of the nations in which the deaths are occurring. Since the West has capability, it has responsibility. You could extend this argument to include other preventable deaths – for example, through military conflict.

Dame Butler-Sloss: Or on the road, by car accidents.

Mr Bains: I think the headline statistic is that there were 1.2 million road traffic accident deaths in the year 2002, which is about 2 per cent of global deaths. It is interesting to note that this was seven times higher than the number of deaths due to military conflict. Most of the traffic accidents took place in India and China, I think.

Dr Smith: I think the question – 'Is the West killing humanity?' – is too much of a generalisation. You could turn it around. Can the West save humanity? Obviously it has a role, but it neither has sole responsibility, nor is it solely capable of doing so. Nevertheless, with the relationships between countries and individuals in a globalised world, there is a responsibility on those of us who live in the West as individuals, communities and nations.

Dame Butler-Sloss: A related question: 'Why is two thirds of the world starving while the other third is trying to lose weight?'

Dr Smith: I count myself among the one third! The question points again to the extraordinary disparities in the world and our continued tolerance of them. A colleague of mine, the Director General of Health in Uganda, was recently speaking at a conference in Africa. He asked the African leaders there why they tolerated the fact that life expectancy in Africa is 20 years lower than anywhere else in the world. How can we talk about this without feeling a sense of extraordinary indignation and anger?

Dame Butler-Sloss: Another related question: 'Why is so much money spent on glamorous medicine of a high-tech nature when so many lives could be saved by simple and affordable treatment?' Mr Bains?

Mr Bains: I think the question was intended to come my way! I am not sure what the questioner meant by 'glamorous medicines', but technology is critical in providing much-needed new medicines, and I don't think there is anything glamorous about that. I think that is capitalising on technological aims for the benefit of health everywhere. Technological gains that are available for diseases of the West can be used for diseases of the developing world.

Simple and affordable medicines *are* available. The WHO has a list of essential drugs, of which there are about 300, of which 95 per cent are non-patented and available cheaply. The issue is not about availability, it is about access. Not enough people have access to a health-care infrastructure of hospitals, clinics and affordable medicines. There are highly effective drugs to cure TB, and yet millions still die of it, because they lack access to a health-care structure that can deliver the medicine to them.

Dr Smith: I think it comes down to choice. People will cite how much money we spend on luxuries such as pet food or cosmetics, and compare it to the amount of money that is spent on health. Clearly, we spend more on our pets in the West than we do on health care in the developing world. The implication of such a comparison is that you can just shift the spending on pets to the developing world. This is naïve. The problem is addressed by the choices we make, not so much as individuals – though that is important – but as communities, nations and at an international level.

Mr Bains has pointed to the fact that health-care infrastructures in many countries are in a state of collapse. Some of this is a result of macro-economic policies that were inflicted on them by international financing institutions in the seventies and eighties, but it is also because of the way the world is working at the moment. We find, for example, that many health workers in Africa are now moving to Europe and to the

Americas. Market forces are moving health workers who are needed in their own countries to other parts of the world, and as a result, many African countries are crying out to stop this flow that is depleting their hospitals and clinics. The problem is thus as much about global institutions and mechanisms as it is about our individual choices.

Archbishop: The question is related to what I was asking earlier about the moral choices that confront people in research, but you have helpfully focused on personnel as a resource as well as material products. Effective infrastructures require trained, committed personnel. Political situations and economic pressures mean that such people are not encouraged or enabled to stay where they need to be. It is paradoxical that nations export medically trained personnel elsewhere when they are needed on the spot. Of course, it may be that the country where they are going is exporting personnel back again. I was in Great Ormond Street Children's Hospital yesterday for a meeting at which some of the staff were describing their own partnerships with medical institutions in Uganda. They were eager to discuss further opportunities of becoming involved in HIV work in Africa, as well as the phenomenal complex of issues around the rehabilitation of abducted child soldiers.

Dame Butler-Sloss: Another question: 'Do intellectual property rights have a negative impact on global health?'

Mr Bains: My answer is 'No.' They have a positive impact on global health. Intellectual property rights are a fundamental for the research and development based industries. Without those rights there would be no incentive to invest the enormous sums of money at high risk over long periods of time that are required if new drugs are to be developed. The rights are needed for the development of new medicines, new cures and new vaccines, not just for the unmet medical needs of today, but for those of tomorrow as well.

There are two illustrations to demonstrate that intellectual property rights do not obstruct health care. The first is the one I've already mentioned. The WHO has a list of just over 300 medicines that are described as essential medicines, that provide basic health-care requirements. Ninety-five per cent of these are non-patented, and yet I think the WHO's own data show that in the developing world access to these medicines can be as low as 50 per cent. Lack of access is the problem, not patenting.

In India, where intellectual property rights have not been available, there is an industrial capacity second to none in manufacturing generic (non-branded) pharmaceuticals. There are 20,000 pharmaceutical manufacturing units in India. And yet the Indian statistics on HIV show that last year fewer than 3 per cent of HIV patients in India are receiving anti-retroviral drugs. That figure is even lower than in Africa. Again, this is not to do with patenting but to do with access.

Dr Smith: I don't think the answer is a simple one. The way that intellectual property rights are exercised can have a profound impact on global health, both in a negative way but also in a very positive way. WHO has been extremely pleased to see developments over the last year with the Doha declaration and the discussions with the World Trade Organisation to clarify how countries can have access to medicines currently under patent. Mechanisms such as voluntary licensing and compulsory licensing can be used, and global agreements such as those we saw at Doha can certainly facilitate increased access to affordable medicines for poor countries.

At the same time it is imperative that we retain a research and development capacity. At the moment, this is primarily funded through the research-based pharmaceutical industry, which relies on profits to continue that work. There is always going to be a need to strike a balance between the demands of the market and the need for public health and public good.

Dame Butler-Sloss: Could we change the focus of the discussion entirely with this question: 'Is there a role for medical missionaries in today's world?'

Dr Smith: I would say that I still am one, so yes! Otherwise, I would be denying both my faith and my calling. Perhaps, however, the nature of medical missionaries has changed quite profoundly over the last 30 or 40 years. When we started in the eighties and just prior to that, there was an assumption that a medical missionary was somebody who went out and worked in a hospital and delivered clinical care to patients who were sick. The majority of people I know, who continue in missions and who come from a medical or a nursing background, are often more involved in providing support to training institutions and development projects in countries, rather than directly giving health care. The other change is away from the view of medical missionaries coming from the West to the poorer countries of the world. Now we see ourselves as sharing experiences. And, of course, much of the mission work taking place is the other way round – people are coming to the former colonial powers as missionaries.

Archbishop: I agree with what has been said. It relates to the way in which institutions, such as Great Ormond Street Hospital, develop partnerships with a focus on training and capacity building. The role of medical missionaries continues to be crucial so long as we continue to hold in clear focus the need to train people in order to build up local resource, not simply to provide from a distance.

Dame Butler-Sloss: The next question: 'Would the panel reflect on the high levels of pressure, resulting in suicide and drug abuse, in the developed world?' Dr Williams?

Archbishop: It is noticeable that there are different levels of suicide in different societies. They are much higher in the developed world. The problems of boredom, of a lack of spiritual purpose, and the pressure in some societies not to be seen to fail – all these affect suicide levels. For me, all these issues are addressed by the religious faith that I hold and profess. This is that there is a constantly unfolding horizon for the heart and spirit of human beings in the infinite love of God. There is always permission to fail because there is always the possibility of a new beginning. These things are so central to the Christian Gospel that I believe they are fundamental to health in the widest sense.

Dr Smith: One of the things that disturbs me is that we have such a low awareness of the burden of mental illness in society as a whole, and also of the burden of mental illness in the developing world. Neuro-psychiatric disorders and mental illness are the third most significant, the third largest burden of disease and disability in the world. It has always been assumed that mental illness is a problem for the West, but it isn't. In many different parts of the world, as societies fragment and crumble, and as families break up, the problem gets worse.

Archbishop: In addition, the mental health legacy of child abductees and conscript soldiers is massive. The trauma for those children in the developing world generally is growing as situations of extreme violence, in which they are made complicit, grow. It is a mental health time-bomb in many African countries.

Dame Butler-Sloss: There are helplines in this country and the Samaritans, for example, do a great deal of good work in providing someone to talk to for those who feel their lives have gone beyond their ability to cope. Is this an area in which the developed countries can help? Could there be private enterprise to help people in this situation, say in Africa?

Archbishop: There are extensive counselling services especially around HIV/AIDS assistance, and now around post-conflict situations. There is work of tremendous imagination which is often much more culturally rooted and locally grown than medical care in the narrower sense, because it grows out of the institutions and community networks that are there. The work still needs intensive resourcing from elsewhere.

Dame Butler-Sloss: Is this to some extent recognised by local churches?

Archbishop: There's no either/or here, because much of the work on education, support and counselling around HIV/AIDS is bound in with faith communities. One example I know of at close quarters is in Uganda. Early on, the Church in Uganda acknowledged the severity of the problem of HIV/AIDS, and the Church's involvement has helped to make the struggle against HIV/AIDS more successful than elsewhere.

Dame Butler-Sloss: Now a highly contentious question: 'Would the panel like to comment on the use of animals in medical research?' I know that people have very strong, differing views on this, and it is important to discuss it objectively.

Mr Bains: In order to develop the much-needed new medicines, cures and vaccines for the unmet medical needs of today and those of tomorrow, we need to have well researched and developed products. Animal testing is in one dimension regrettable, but in another it is necessary to demonstrate the activity of pharmaceutical compounds. Indeed, the regulations require animal testing if products are to be given government licenses for marketing. Clearly, the pharmaceutical industry wants to limit the extent to which animal testing happens. Indeed, it is embarked on extensive assessments of alternative models to achieve the same pharmacokinetic dynamic end-points that can be tested in animal models. I would also say that the animals that are used in the necessary experiments are bred for that purpose, and every measure is taken to ensure the dignity of the animals and the limitation of their suffering.

Archbishop: It's another of those issues on which general public awareness has shifted over the decades. I think the intensity with which the question is now asked has grown. A while ago there would have been less unease. While I find it difficult to be absolutist about this, I am relieved to know of explorations into alternative methods, because it seems to me that respect for the human self and respect for the living environment are very closely allied. There really is a limit to how much you can exploit the living environment if you don't want to damage your sense of yourself.

Dr Smith: Thought has shifted more broadly on the ethics of medical research over the last 20 years. It had been assumed, though this was never written down anywhere, that ethical standards were a national issue. Therefore, if the ethical standards in one country were lower than in another, and you could do your research more cheaply and easily in the country with lower standards, that is where you went to do your research. Now there is a recognition of ethical standards being more universal than that, and that it would be inequitable to apply different standards around the world, because that would denigrate the value of human life.

Dame Butler-Sloss: This is the last question we have time for: 'Is it healthier to be a person of faith than not?' Dr Williams?

Archbishop: Not so easy to answer, actually. There is some research that suggests that people who have a living religious faith have correspondingly favourable life-expectancy. But God forbid that I should try to market religious faith as a way of having a longer life! There's a long history in all faith traditions, not least in Christianity, of saying that it is neither here nor there whether religious faith makes your life easier. The question is, is the religion true? In other words, is it good for you in that global and indeed eternal sense? At that level I would say, yes, of course it is healthier to be a person of faith. But it won't save you from the common cold.

Dame Butler-Sloss: Could I now ask each of our speakers to say a few words in summary and conclusion?

Mr Bains: The evening's dialogue has been interesting and provocative. We've covered a broad terrain including all the key elements of global health. My view is that the jury is still out on whether humanity is killing itself. We have the capacity to do much more damage to ourselves than we are currently. With the mobilisation of political will and public and private enterprise, however, we have the capability to ensure that the answer to the question becomes an unequivocal 'No.'

Dr Smith: I ended my introductory statement by saying that I thought humanity wasn't killing all of itself, only the poorest parts. I'd like to finish tonight by looking at what can be done about that. There are three things. One is to recognise the right to health, and to make it clear that health is not just about drugs and vaccines, it's inherently about equity and social justice. I think it was Kofi Annan who said his aspiration was that health will finally be seen not as a blessing to be wished for but a human right to be fought for. The second thing to do is to move from rhetoric to real action, starting with honouring international commitments to overseas development assistance. The third thing to do is for each of us to choose to live a healthy lifestyle – and as my wife reminds me, I need to lose some weight!

Archbishop: Mine too! We've been reminded several times

tonight of the inseparable link between health and power and resource in the world. It is entirely right and proper that there is no distinction in the classical and biblical languages between health and salvation. My faith tells me that the body is a good gift of God which must be treasured and nurtured. It demands of us the deepest possible respect, and therefore the deepest possible investment of skill, understanding and imagination. Set that in the context of justice and welfare for all, and I think you see how the Gospel, as I would put it, has to be realised among us.

Dame Butler-Sloss: Thank you very much. Thank you to all our dialogue participants, and thank you to our audience for your attention and excellent questions. Good night.

Afterword

by Dr Rowan Williams, Archbishop of Canterbury

One of the things that emerged most clearly from the dialogues was the impossibility of separating the four problems we were talking about from each other. Underlying all the discussions is, I think, one particular set of issues that has to do with trust and consent. In George Monbiot's phrase, everything has been globalised except consent. We have no system of world governance as such; rather we have a single vastly resourced superpower which can mould the destinies of other nations both by economic pressure and by military intervention – and which can make a massive difference also by opting out of international systems, economic, ecological or legal. It may be (as Professor Bobbitt argues in the first of the dialogues) that the USA has no strictly imperial ambitions, and that its presence in various contexts depends on the consent of a host society. But its influence is so vast and its recent military initiatives so forceful that it is naïve to think that it does or even can act as a benevolent elder sibling or a helpful and disinterested guest. The question of consent is inescapable here. And the sort of reform of the UN and its agencies that plays so important a part in the thinking of many –

like Lord Owen – seems unlikely, of itself alone, to resolve these issues of trust.

This is partly because of the economic structures which determine the lives of smaller nations, making them vulnerable to protectionism from wealthier countries, destabilisation because of unregulated capital flow and debt, and what might be called civic degradation, the erosion of civil society, as a result of 'rationalisation' imposed by outside agencies. Dr Yunus makes out a powerful case for trusting local co-operative ventures and changing the law in various countries to enable better micro-credit facilities; the co-operative principle needs reinforcing by aid policies and by the World Bank, not least because local and co-operative credit structures have so good a record of not creating impossible spirals of indebtedness. Professor Kay shows more optimism about the self-renewing capacity of market economies and about the ability of the market in the long run to deliver the best results in development. But he is careful to stress that economics does not work in a vacuum, and that the lack of practices and institutions that nurture trust is one of the things that in fact cripple the effective growth of the market. Both agree that a stronger alliance between conventional banking and micro-credit needs forging if trust is not to go on being a casualty of market systems.

The finite nature of what economics can work on is a backdrop to the third dialogue. Our resources are not inexhaustible; pretending they are is the legacy of a bizarre mythology separating humanity from the 'natural' world and glorifying dominance and control. Dr Midgley and Dr Navarro both underline the degree to which the ecological irresponsibility of much of historic capitalism is bound up with a cheapening of human life. If we cannot respect our environment, we are less likely to respect humanity, more likely to reinforce wide-ranging systems of control which once again ignore questions about consent. And one index of proper trust in ourselves and our capacity to change things is how seriously we take even the smallest steps towards greater responsibility in our personal lives. Globally, we need with desperate urgency a dependable – trustworthy – system of regulation and adjustment of the 'freedom' to pollute. This should be a major political priority for our own and every government; making it so depends on a shift of public interest, the generating of some real passion about the world in which we are not aliens but full participants.

Trust, consent and taking responsibility for our fate belong together. Pervading the last of the dialogues was a concern about how people could come to believe that they had some real control over their actual physical health, given the way in which economics can limit the development of a viable infrastructure for health care in poorer nations (and indeed in poorer regions of more prosperous countries), and given also the record of some of the pharmaceutical industry. Mr Bains mounted an eloquent defence of his own company's more recent record and emphasised the importance of building up local capacity to deliver. Dr Smith noted the potential of the proposed International Finance Facility in this connection; and both echoed the concern to change the level of public motivation about this. It was abundantly clear that the developed world was held responsible for hugely disproportionate damage to the environment, and that health questions could not intelligibly be addressed without making the connection again and again with the previous week's subject matter. And the mental health of the world appeared on the horizon as a shared concern – both the unimaginable traumas of those, especially children, caught up in the deprivation of the disadvantaged world, and the boredom, cynicism and depression characteristic of an over-stimulated Western culture.

The wounds that currently make our world suffer so greatly are not to be healed in a few weeks or even a few years. No one in any of these dialogues had a comprehensive short-term strategy to resolve the issues raised. But no one was very satisfied with how things stood. It is obvious that there is a deficit of trust in a world where it is widely perceived that effective decisions lie with a tiny minority. If global institutions of any kind – multinationals, UN agencies, NGOs – are to do anything, they have to operate in a way that makes clearly visible the presence and the interest of all parties involved. The crises we looked at in the dialogues often reduce themselves to crises of *legitimacy*: by what possible right are decisions taken by those who currently take them, if their only title is sheer economic or military resource? So improving the representative character of the Security Council, putting an International Finance Facility in place, tightening regulation of capital flow and resisting the pressure for blanket economic 'liberalisation' in developing countries, relaxing the law around micro-credit, giving incentives to drug companies to offer discounted supplies where they are needed, and being willing as a society to challenge mantras about economic growth here in the name of ecological and economic responsibility – all these have to be held together as a response to the same underlying question, 'By what right is the world run as it is?' Without inclusion and enabling, we are condemned to a future of deepening alienation and the endemic violence that goes with it.

In each of the dialogues, it was also clear that the questions demanded answers that drew on the heritage of religious faith. They are not to be answered as if we could simply decide in the abstract what sort of things human beings were. We need a vision of the truth about humanity, a vision we cannot work out by unaided human capacity. There should be no embarrassment in saying that the Gospel addresses each of the questions we considered at its root. The Gospel tells us that anxious fear of God and each other is the heart of our selfishness and obsessive acquisitiveness. It tells us that we shall all die and face judgement and that no amount of acquisition can save us from this. But it also tells us that we are loved and trusted by our Creator, who has put the divine life itself at our disposal by living in our midst and thus earning our trust. Because of what he has done, we do not have to live in anxiety, controlled by the passions of competition for scarce resources; we can live in a 'body' whose fundamental law is that the welfare (or poverty or suffering) of each is the welfare (or poverty or suffering) of all. We are given a gift – faith, trustful living – that changes every aspect of the world we see and belong to. At the very least, if we are to confront the world's agonies with honesty and without despair, we have somehow to find ground on which to stand with trust; if we do, and if we are formed into that body where there is no such thing as a purely individual interest, issues of trust and legitimacy resolve themselves.

The dialogues were in no way designed as an exercise in Christian apologetic; but they did repeatedly uncover matters on which the Christian Gospel has a perspective not always heard clearly in a culture that has largely forgotten where its moral orientation comes from. It is significant that a great church like St Paul's can still be a forum, in a very literal sense – a public space where citizens can debate issues that go beyond narrow electoral politics. Our society needs such spaces as much as ever, perhaps more when we consider the extreme gravity and urgency of all that these evenings touched upon. I am personally profoundly grateful to all at St Paul's who facilitated the dialogues, and those who generously gave time to chair them. My hope, and that of all my conversation partners, is that they may stimulate some real shifts in our motivation as we struggle to make our world a place where power feels legitimate, where it is possible to trust strangers, where we are able to believe that what moves and affects each of us is genuinely heard and under- stood by all.